BAD CHOICES MAKE GOOD STORIES

CONVERSATIONS ABOUT WRITING

ERIN M. DIONNE

Foreword by
KAREN BOSS

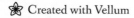

For Annette, Danielle, Gary, Megan, Phoebe, and Wendy:

I couldn't do this without you.

CONTENTS

FOREWORD

In this collection of essays, so delightfully called *Bad Choices*, author Erin Dionne talks about shortcuts and magic several times. She writes at one point, "There are no shortcuts; no magic." While it is absolutely true that there are no shortcuts in writing, I'll fight Erin any day about the magic. There is magic. It's you—the writer. You're the magic.

I've been a book editor for nine years now. And I've been a book reader for more than four decades. No matter which hat I'm wearing when I read a book or manuscript, I always wonder how the writer did it. How did this person create something so good? So nuanced? So funny? So poignant? As a non-writer, I have no idea. I can only assume it's magic.

I've been privileged to work with Erin as her editor on two picture books. She knows what she's doing and what she's talking about. You should listen to her and reap the amazing advice she has to share through this collection of essays.

I often struggle with the fact that publishing lives in a weird place where creativity and commerce intersect. And since Erin loves a good analogy, I'll offer one here.

You've been driving down Creativity Avenue for a while. You're getting to know the road with all its twists and turns. You've found a good speed and figured out what the ten-and-two position on the wheel looks like for you. You've finally accepted that there are no shortcuts.

Now you're coming up on Manuscript-Finished Lane, and you're maybe even going to turn on Get-an-Agent Boulevard. You're suddenly aware that Commerce Street is fast approaching. All of this is what *Bad Choices* is for. How do you balance writing and publishing? Find both critique and community? Make time and make money? Work for both life and livelihood?

Don't worry. Erin is here to help. And since she's an author too, keep your eye out for a little magic on the side of the road.

—Karen Boss, editor at Charlesbridge Publishing and believer in the magic of writers

WHAT'S AN ATHOR, ANYWAY?

Let's talk.

━━━

When I was in second grade, I filled out a worksheet about what I wanted to be when I grew up. In purple crayon, I wrote "An Athor."

Spelling was not my strong suit, okay?

I was—and still am—an avid reader. But I didn't know what An Athor did, exactly. I had no idea how books were made or how people wrote them. I just loved stories.

As I got older, I did not constantly scribble in notebooks or tell tales to my stuffed animals, although I kept the occasional diary. Honestly, I participated in music programs as much, if not more than, the literary magazines at school. But the fascination with stories and reading stayed with me. How did writers create those fictional places that I inhabited and loved so much? Could I do that, too? Could I be a writer?

To try and find out, I went to college and majored in English. Then, I added a communications major because it seemed practical. I took a bunch of literature classes and wrote a lot of papers about the books I read (because that's evidently what English majors did: read books and write papers), and peppered in creative writing courses when I could add them to my schedule. In those classes, I wrote some clunky short stories about characters I didn't know and (adult) lives I didn't understand.

By my senior year, I understood how to take a story apart and talk about it. I could analyze structure and tone, discuss voice and symbols. My communications major gave me practical writing skills (press releases, marketing materials) and public speaking experience.

But I couldn't get my own stories on paper the way I envisioned in my head. I certainly didn't feel like a writer, and although I read a lot of stories and understood how they worked, I hadn't actually *written* very much.

When I graduated, I wanted to learn how to write. Enter: Graduate school. I got a job in a bookstore and went to Emerson College for a Master of Fine Arts in creative writing. Not far into the academic year, I left the bookstore for a temporary position at Houghton Mifflin publishers, which turned into a full-time job marketing math textbooks.

I had health insurance, a salary, and night classes. In grad school, I also did the thing that I hadn't done as an English major: I wrote stories...many unpublishable stories. And then a registration mishap led me to enroll in a writing for children class—and *that's* when writing actually clicked for me. Those stories that I read as a kid came flooding back. I remembered the voracious reader I'd been as a child and the books I'd loved. In class, we explored current children's books, and I fell in love with the characters and novels the same way I had as a ten-year-old. I devoured books for kids. Those awkward, awful years of middle school were filled with potential for characters and problems. I couldn't wait to get those on the page. I found my voice.

My stories featuring adult characters were stilted, boring, and inauthentic. The ones for kids were probably still stilted and boring, but the voice was there, which made them less terrible and more authentic. Writing for, and about, kids, made sense to me. I had a specific direction for my craft.

There were other pieces that came together. At my day job, I met a colleague who was a poet, and then another one who was a short story writer. The short story writer led me to a writing group that met after hours in a conference room on the sixth floor of our building. The poet and I supported one another in our quest for publication, setting goals and becoming one another's cheerleaders. We put together a community reading series and a company literary magazine. Having others around me who prioritized their writing was a revelation. Being a writer always seemed like a solo endeavor, but it didn't have to be. I had a piece of flash fiction published, and one of my short stories won a local writing prize. Being part of a community of creators became critical to my work.

But I still didn't *feel* like a writer.

I didn't have a book published. Writing was hard, making time to write was hard, and movies and books made it seem like writing was easy if you were really, truly into it.

Was I really, truly into it?

I left the publisher and went to work for a magazine as an editor, lost that job in the dot com bust, and then fell into teaching. I got married. A couple of years of adjunct work led me to a small art college north of Boston, where I took over their academic support office and taught classes. I built a family. Then I became part of the college's full-time faculty. I've been there ever since, teaching creative writing and literature courses to art students. Through that, I kept writing. I stayed connected and active in my writing community. I learned about the publishing industry. I surrounded myself with people who took their art-making seriously.

Along the way, I started taking my own writing more seriously: I began attending conferences to continue learning about craft. I signed with an agent, who sold my first book for tweens in 2007. I published seven novels and two picture books, had essays and stories accepted to anthologies, and presented at the conferences I attended when I was starting out. I expanded my speaking to national conferences for teachers, visited schools and libraries across the country to talk about books and writing, and have been fortunate to meet many wonderful people who create books for kids.

What I've found is that writing is still hard, making time to write is still hard, and everyone's "really, truly into it" looks completely different—but that's all part of being An Athor. It's a unique path for each of us.

When I put it down on paper, I realize that I've literally spent more than half of my life reading, writing, analyzing, and talking about stories. I understand how publishing works; I know how to juggle a day job and writing and take care of small children. I don't claim to be an expert, but I am an expert in my own experience, which I can share. I'm finally ready to own the Athor label.

So, is this a craft book? Encouragement and support for those who are stuck or feeling as though they don't have what it takes? A meditation on why write in the first place?

Yes to all of those things.

Here are some ways to go about being An Athor.

CRAFT

CHAPTER 1

THE TOOLBOX

WRITING IS ALL ABOUT TRIAL AND ERROR, TESTING AND trying, poking at something, trying it a different way, holding it up to the light, turning it a little, then trying something different.

Just like any other artist, writers have tools that we work with as we use our craft. We learn about structure and dialogue, character development and pacing. We talk about strong openings and effective endings, point of view and perspective. Having a space to contain our tools is important.

Creatively, building a toolbox matters. Stephen King talks a bit about his toolbox in his book *On Writing*. The nuggets we learn from a conference, or a bit that we take from a talk, we drop into a tray in our box. We may not use that info right now, but it'll be there for us when we need it.

A writer friend told me that every time you write a book, it's like you've never done it before. The drafting process that worked the first time, or the previous ten times, is likely not going to be the process that works for this particular story. I remember scoffing internally. I had a *creative process* for writing my first published book. I *figured it out.*

Ha. The universe scoffed at *me* when I started my second book, which became *The Total Tragedy of a Girl Named Hamlet.* Forget process—it was like I hadn't even used a keyboard before! I rewrote the opening three chapters five times. I couldn't find a plot to save my life. I didn't understand how to bring the story together.

Humbling, for sure.

This is where the toolbox comes in. There's never a "right way" to create—whether you're writing, painting, or sculpting. There are best practices, and ways that have worked in the past, but every individual act of creation needs something unique. Part of the creative process is figuring out what that *thing* is. Having access to the tools we've accumulated helps us in those moments when we're stuck.

Creatively learning and growing is critical. You are not the same writer you were five years ago, and your books should reflect that. As our experience grows, our books change. Every so often, I come across a writer who believes they don't need to go to conferences or learn from other writers. I don't understand that reluctance. We can always learn from one another, and even if you've heard someone talk about a process point or approach before, chances are it's going to apply to your work differently now.

King was speaking metaphorically about his toolbox, but I have a literal digital toolbox: For the past several years, I've been keeping notes from talks, conferences, or craft conversations in the app Evernote. This app allows me to categorize broad subjects as "notebooks," then post documents into the corresponding notebook. I can tag each note for easier searching. For example, I can search "character," and 130 notes come up. Or, I can look in particular notebooks—such as The New England Society of Children's Book Writers and Illustrators—for notes that I take at that conference every year. Evernote is my digital toolbox.

You don't need something digital—a lined notebook (maybe one with subject dividers) works just as well.

The most important aspect is developing a dedicated space that works for you to house your tools. I'm not going to remember everything I learn, and this way, I can go back and look for something to make sure I have it right. Also, when the writing isn't going so well, or when I'm between projects, I can read through those notes and brush up on tips. Something in there may spark just what I need for the next project.

Whether metaphorical, physical, or digital, the tools of the craft deserve their own space. What do you use as your toolbox?

CHAPTER 2

ON KEEPING A NOTEBOOK

(WITH THANKS TO JOAN DIDION)

▭

ONE OF THE items I've found to be most valuable in my writing life is a notebook. I am a notebook...collector (sounds better than "hoarder", doesn't it?).

The notebook is the first place my ideas land. When I decide that something is worthy of pursuit, it goes into a notebook, where I can work out the details of the idea before setting it to laptop.

I have notebooks of all shapes and sizes, some of which were given as gifts years ago that are waiting for the just right project. I prefer spiral bound, lines on the front, blank on the back, but the project usually dictates the right notebook. For example, when I was writing *Ollie and the Science of Treasure Hunting,*

I used a black graph paper/grid lined notebook because that's the same type of notebook that the main character uses in the story.

When I give talks, I tell people that the cover of my notebooks usually connect with my story somehow. That's true, although not entirely so. It honestly makes it sound *less* woo-woo than it actually is. I typically get a feeling about the notebook—so picture me, wandering aisles and browsing websites, until something lights up for me. There! It's the "just right notebook" for that story. When I see it, I *know*. There's a level of comfort and satisfaction when I've chosen the "right" place to develop this story—it's almost as though there's a psychological element clicking into place, and my brain knows the work can actually begin.

So what is it for, exactly? How does one use a notebook? For some writer friends, their notebooks are repositories for everything they are thinking, and they toss ideas into the same space, willy-nilly. To me, that's a little like a crowded closet. How can you find anything in there?

I have several active notebooks: One, I've turned in to a bullet journal, for my to-do lists, schedules, etc. One is a general repository for writing stuff—notes from conferences and the like. Two are personal journals, and then there's my project notebook. There are times when I think that I have too many notebooks, but...nah.

Twyla Tharp famously begins choreography projects with a box.

My project notebook is my box.

Once I've settled on the notebook, I make sure to date the inside cover, so I can track how long each project takes. Then I use the notebook for that project, exclusively.

BRAINSTORMING AND PREWRITING

The notebook is the place where I do all of the prewriting on my novels. It takes me a few months of working the story out by hand before I start writing on the machine. By prewriting, I mean making lists of character traits, bubble diagrams (or webs) of plot ideas, writing letters in my characters' voices...working out the "what ifs" of the story. Having the connection between my brain and my hand, plus the freedom to literally draw what I need to (a map, a chart, a calendar, a sketch), helps the story take shape for me.

Typically, I also add a pocket to the inside back cover, if the notebook I'm using doesn't already have one. The pocket is where I stick those bits of info that I collect on the (rare) occasion I don't have the notebook with me. Or the ephemera I collect during the research process—a brochure, a photo or cutout from a magazine, etc. The pocket keeps everything for me, neatly.

There comes a point, usually after about three to four months when prewriting on a novel, when I'm ready to start writing. I have a handle on the main character, I know what their issues are and what they are struggling with, and I understand where the story is going.

I begin.

But I'm not done with the notebook.

During the Writing Process

Even when I'm drafting on the machine, I still use the notebook.

During times when I'm struggling (and, when I'm drafting, those are many), I set a 15-minute timer and do a freewrite to get my head clear and ready for the story. That freewriting happens in the notebook. Sometimes it's a mewling, complainy, whiney, "poor me" freewrite. Sometimes I'm just making a glorified to do list, so I can clear work and life out of my head, to make space for the story. Sometimes, the freewrite is all about plot issues. It doesn't matter. I likely won't read it again. It's just to get my hand going and nudge my brain into the right gear for writing and imaginative work.

When I'm drafting, if I get stuck on a plot problem, I work it out and play with options in the notebook—or I go back through the prewriting I've done. Frequently, I'll find a solution to a problem. If I want to keep track of something, like a character's eye color, or their class schedule for school, it goes in the notebook. Anything that needs consistency and is recurring goes in the notebook.

Critiquing and Revision

Once I'm into the draft a little, and I know where I'm going, I may be ready to share what I have with my critique group. When we meet—whether virtually or in-person—I take notes about the conversation in my notebook. I write each person's name with a colon (Gary:) and make a bulleted list of their feedback. Having the hand-brain connection ensures I remember what they've said, and it also gives me a functional document to work from when I start my revision process.

Once that draft is done, I print the manuscript and go through the whole thing by hand. I use the notebook to organize my to-do list for the revision, so I can methodically check off what changes I've made as I work.

That's a Wrap—Not

Only when the book has gone through copyedits do I retire that notebook—meaning, I no longer add material about that story to that notebook. Instead, I add the date to the inside of the front cover and stick it on the shelf next to the others from previous novels. But even when the book is published, the notebook is not forgotten. I frequently take notebooks off my shelf to show students aspects of my writing process, and sometimes I'll go back and look at how a project evolved before I put together a talk for a conference or school visit.

The notebook is old-school, low-tech, and not for everyone. Maybe it will work for you, but maybe you prefer the

Notes app on your phone, or a Word doc, or some such. Whatever appeals to you—go for it. The point is to have a dedicated space for the work associated with each project. This saves you time, helps you develop materials that you need, and serves as a record of the process that it takes for you to complete each book.

CHAPTER 3

BAD CHOICES MAKE GOOD STORIES: CREATING CHARACTERS

Our main characters are the central element around which our story revolves. For me, with rare exceptions, they are the place where story begins. I think of a character first, and then develop the world, problems, and plot around that person.

As I'm building my characters, I always ask: How do I create compelling characters who our readers will want to follow in their journeys?

Creating characters requires thinking about and developing this person until they come to life off the page. There are steps to creating this person, whether we identify those steps consciously or not. In this section, I am going to pull apart those steps and show how they work for me.

THE BASICS

Imagine a wire-framed mannequin, like the kind you'd find in a trendy boutique. They have a height and shape but are featureless. We can give them a name and some general traits: brown eyes, blue hair. Perhaps we know their age, occupation, superficial information about their background, and basic likes and dislikes. By the time we're done, we can see them, they can walk around a little, but if we question them too deeply, they'll run out of things to say. I started drafting my sixth novel, *Lights, Camera, Disaster,* before I had a deep understanding of the main character—I figured I had enough experience to wing it. Wrong! After about twenty-five pages, I got stuck. Hess, the main character, wasn't fully formed, and I couldn't figure out what she would do in certain situations. So I went back to my brainstorming stage and spent more time developing her. It was a good reminder that spending the time to learn about my character during the brainstorming stage pays off when I'm drafting.

INTERNAL MACHINATIONS

In my notebook, I take that dressed-up basic character frame and start filling its insides. What does this person want in their life? What do they need? Wants and needs are different. *Wants* are something that the character can tell you (or another character) about. They *know* they want this thing. Wants could be as concrete as a new bike, or a better job, or a pet, or to do well in school. They could also want a friend, or a way out of their town. The important thing is that the character knows what it is, so they can go after it.

Needs are holes inside the character that must be filled. Characters likely *can't* articulate their need to you (or someone else in the story) at the beginning of the book. In order for the character to fulfill their need, they have to experience the events of the story. By the end, their need is addressed, and their life is different. Sometimes, they can't articulate what their need is at the end of the book, either—but they are happy and satisfied, even if they don't know why.

The Rolling Stones gave us important lyrics about wants and needs (come on, you know the words). Your character doesn't have to achieve their want, but they really do have to get their needs met. A character's journey of trying to get what they want helps them to discover, and fill, that need. In *Notes from an Accidental Band Geek*, my third novel, the main character Elsie *wants* to be a professional French horn player—but she *needs* friends. Her struggles with marching band illustrate how her life grows richer when she lets people in.

Wants and needs make up only a portion of the material inside our character. Characters must have a personality. They need to be *active*. Our characters have to make decisions and choices that propel the story forward.

I'll say it again: *Our characters have to make decisions and choices that propel the story forward.* This is what we mean by active vs. passive characters. Active characters go after the thing that they want, which causes them to make decisions, and those decisions affect the plot. Passive characters, on the other hand, let life happen to them. Circumstance, not choice, dictates what is going on in a passive character's story. As a result, the plot plods, the character doesn't grow, and the writer ends up stuck.

With an active character, the story ends up feeling more organic, because the plot points are coming from the character's actions. A passive character forces the writer to institute obstacle after obstacle, which causes the story to feel manufactured and the reader to subsequently lose interest.

Lastly, those choices made by active characters can't just be binary good/bad choices. That's too easy. For example: your teen character gets grounded, but there's a party on Saturday night that they are dying to attend. You could set up a choice where the character a.) stays home and accepts their punishment, or b.) sneaks out to go to the party. *Yawn.* There is a clear "good" and "bad" choice here—and of course your character is going to sneak out, because that makes the better story. But it's too obvious of a decision point. Instead, set up *two bad choices*: your teen character gets grounded, but there's a party on Saturday night that they are dying to attend. This character is going to go, regardless. The choice then becomes: a.) Will they sneak out and meet their friend down at the end of the street? or b.) Will they sneak out, borrow their mom's car, and pick up their friend?

I know which one I'm choosing.

Bad choices make good stories. Our characters need to learn from their mistakes in order to grow. It's up to us as writers to do them the favor of giving them experiences to learn from. When our characters choose between two bad options, it immediately heightens the tension and gives readers something to be invested in.

EXTERNAL FORCES

We've fleshed out that wire frame, dressing it on the outside and giving it an inner life and poor decision-making skills. Should be all set, right? Nope. The last element we need to truly bring our character to life is *other characters*. I have a selection in this book on developing minor characters, so I won't spend a long time on this. But the important point is that we think about how our main character behaves in relation to other people. In real life, we have different kinds of relationships with our boss, coworkers, friends, spouse, children, baristas, etc. A lot of those relationships are dependent upon power differentials. How does your character behave when they interact with someone who has more power than they do? Or power over them? How does your character behave in a situation when they have power over someone else?

When you figure out how these external forces work on your main character, they will truly come to life—bad choices and all.

CHAPTER 4

PROMISES, PROMISES

Beginnings are important. The opening of a story is what hooks the reader into the world you've built, and gets them to engage with your character.

Even before we get to the reader portion of the program, a strong beginning hooks agents, gets the attention of contest judges, and gets editors excited. Beginnings have a lot of work to do. They:

• Introduce the main character and their situation

• Set up the problem that the book or main character will be dealing with

• Set the voice or tone of the piece

• Orient the reader to the world in a fantasy or sci-fi piece.

This is a big list! Beginnings have a heavy lift, which is why I go back to mine over and over again during my drafting and revision processes.

Some of my novels had the same essential beginning from the draft to final product (Models, Band Geek, and Fangirl). Others have had multiple iterations before I've settled on the beginning. All of them have gone through edits and shifts by the time I completed a draft. Your beginning likely will change as well, since it's nearly impossible to get the beginning spotless before finishing the ending.

All of this aside, the craft element that I want to focus on regarding beginnings is the idea of The Promise.

The beginning of any story sets up expectations for the reader: This is going to be a mystery, or a horror novel. This book is going to be funny, or sad, or set in a fantastical world with magic. Readers are savvy, and our brains are wired to look for and pick up clues when we enter a story. As we pick up the clues, we build expectations.

The sky is purple at high noon? This is a fantasy.

That guy can fly? There's magic in this book.

These examples are blatant, but readers' brains pick up subtle clues, too:

That character keeps fiddling with their hat. Hat is important.

The dog gives a sidelong glance that's oddly human. Dog is special, maybe magic.

Once those expectations are set, it becomes hard to shake them. This is why going back to revise our beginnings once we reach the end of our drafts is critical: What are we promising our readers?

I explain this at conferences, and inevitably get the person who says, "But I want to surprise my readers! The magic in my book doesn't get revealed until page 87."

My response is always this: "Have you ever seen a movie trailer, and then gone to the movie and experienced something totally different? You thought it was going to be funnier, or scary, or... whatever? Remember that feeling of frustration and annoyance? *That* is the feeling you do *not* want your reader to have."

If we have been led to believe that we are reading a realistic fiction novel, and then all of a sudden there's giant mutant spiders—with no warning, clues, or expectation that they are coming—your reader would likely throw that book across the room. My guess is that this behavior is not what you want from your readership.

In general, we do not like bait-and-switch stories.

Yes, there are exceptions. But...I'll also add that a lot of the exceptions have actually subtly laid the foundation for that bait-and-switch moment, so you can look back through the beginning of the story and go, "Ahhhh! Yes! THIS was how that was done! I just missed it!"

Our goal as writers is for readers to want to keep reading—we need to make it hard for them to put down that book. It becomes ten times easier for our audience to walk away from a story that is not delivering on their expectations.

Here's how you identify the promise that your book is making to the reader:

• Jot down your vision of the book: A psychological thriller that keeps readers on the edge of their seats. A sweeping romance that takes readers to another place and time. A gothic horror novel that will force readers to keep the lights on at night.

• Go back and read through your first fifty or so pages. Make a list of what is laid out: A tense opening that ratchets up the anxiety? Have you set up a mystery? Is there a hint of romance for that lonely character? Knowing what message you're actually sending, vs. what you want to send, is important.

This is also a great opportunity for your critique group or critique partner to help you out. Once you're done with your draft—or at least you're a good chunk of the way through it— ask one of your trusted critiquers to look at your beginning and tell you what expectations you've set and what promises your book is making. The information you receive can help you lay the groundwork for your revision plan.

Once we make those promises to our readers, we need to deliver on them by the end of our novels—which we'll discuss in another essay. In the meantime, if you clearly identify the promises you're making, you'll have readers who are eager to join you on your story's journey.

CHAPTER 5

FRENEMIES, BARISTAS, AND BUS DRIVERS: NOT-SO MINOR CHARACTERS

MAIN CHARACTERS GET LOTS OF ATTENTION, BUT THEY ARE not the only people populating our stories. Our story worlds contain best friends, relatives, teachers, baristas, bus drivers, frenemies, and all sorts of other roles and personalities. Those characters deserve just as much attention as our main character —for without them, our characters exist in a void.

I learned about writing effective minor characters the hard way. When I wrote my first novel, *Models Don't Eat Chocolate Cookies*, I had a strong story, good voice, great protagonist...and minor characters that were flat cutouts in comparison. The only purpose they served was for my main character to bounce off, much like the studs in a pinball machine. I spent so much time developing Celeste, the main character, that the rest were basically sticks with heads on them.

My then-editor, Alisha Niehaus, helped me to figure out how to develop strong minor characters. She forced me to think of their stories, to tease out their history and relevant information throughout the manuscript. One of the best pieces of advice that she gave me was that our minor characters are stars in their own stories—but we're not reading that book. So every time your minor characters come on stage, we should learn something new about them and their story. Sprinkling that information throughout the manuscript helps build that character in your readers' mind, and as a result they feel more real.

For example: In my book *The Total Tragedy of a Girl Named Hamlet*, we first learn that Hamlet's friend Eli has a big dumb Labrador named Bunny. Later, we find out that Bunny is Eli's sister's dog. Then we find out that Bunny was her gift for completing treatment for leukemia some years back. She's okay, and now they have this dog that Eli has to chase after all the time.

In my novel *Lights, Camera, Disaster*, Hess's friend Nev is dealing with separated parents, and she is *not* happy about it. So she lugs *everything* between their two houses, instead of leaving stuff with each parent, because she wants to remind them that divorce is easy on them, but hard for her (she has a vindictive streak, that Nev). Each time we see her, she's shuttling from one house to the other, and we're learning about her journey in accepting her parents' divorce.

Since I took the time to develop these characters, readers connect with them, and I receive email about them, which is pretty awesome. Another example of a well-drawn minor character is Prim, in the *Hunger Games* trilogy. She begins as a character whom Katniss feels she must protect at all costs, because she can't survive in this world. But due to Katniss's choice to go to the arena, Prim launches on her own journey of becoming a healer and learning medicine. She is the reason that Katniss does what she does, but they *both* grow and change from those actions.

As you're looking at the minor characters in your own work, here are some items to consider:

Beware stock minor characters. The "long-suffering best friend" and the "evil henchman" are examples of these. We see them over and over in literature, and they feel predictable and tired.

Avoid characters who perform one function. They might be the advice-giver, cheerleader, complainer, clue-giver, etc. People aren't one-dimensional and do more for their friends than just provide one skill. It's reductive. This is also a trap that writers can fall into when writing about people of color. There are tropes: the Magical Negro, the Exotic Asian, the Fiery Latina...don't fall into those patterns. They are not reflective of the world we live in and do a disservice to your readership.

Avoid telling everything at once. We use terms like "evolve" when it comes to storytelling for a reason. We need to remember that stories are organic, and it's necessary for information to be revealed slowly, over time. You can't know everything about that woman in the coffee shop just because you shared a table for fifteen minutes. Neither should your reader.

Remember: *Everyone is the star of their own story.* Your minor character is only "minor" in the context of *this* story world, not their own. They've got their own stuff going on. Creating strong minor characters fleshes out the story and provides additional opportunities for discovery from readers. This is another way for your readers to get hooked into your world.

I also like what John Truby says about minor characters:

The biggest mistake writers make...is that they think of the hero and all other characters as separate individuals. The result is...cardboard opponents and minor characters who are even weaker. To create great characters, think of all your characters as part of a web in which each helps define the others.

...Each time you compare a character to your hero, you force yourself to distinguish the hero in new ways. You also start to see the secondary characters as complete human beings, as complex and valuable as your hero.

THE ANATOMY OF STORY. FABER & FABER, 2007. PG. 57.

He goes on to give this elaborate explanation for how characters function, label archetypes, etc. What I believe all of this boils down to is: Are your minor characters going to help the main character achieve his goal? If so, how? If not, how are they going to hinder him? Thinking of your minor characters this way automatically makes them more interesting and engaging. If they have a specific purpose, we as authors then need to use them.

Aside from how these characters support or hinder your main character, you can use them as balance in plot. For example, follow an intense scene with a more comedic one with a lesser character. Or let your minor characters act as a foil by giving them a characteristic that directly contradicts one held by the main character. When they inevitably clash, we can see how your main character grows.

The more attention we pay to these minor characters, the less minor they become. Although they aren't taking the center stage in your story, they are confident enough to walk off your page and into their own world, and readers will respond to that every time.

CHAPTER 6

"RECALIBRATING": FINDING THE CORE OF YOUR STORY

YEARS AGO, I READ A BLOG POST BY YOUNG ADULT AUTHOR Maggie Stiefvater, where she wrote about "the core of the story" in relation to her book, *The Scorpio Races*. The post cracked my writing world wide open, as it gave words to something that I'd sensed about writing, but hadn't, until then, been able to articulate. I started speaking about it with writer friends, digging deeper into my own work, and discussing it with students. Finding the core of your story has become the central part of my practice as a writer.

So what is the core?

Maggie says, "Core is what your novel is. It's not what your novel is about. It's the thing that made you want to tell this story and no other. It's the theme, or the character, or the setting that made you love it. You have to know what the specific core of your novel is, because that's all that you're going to consider sacred."

Let's unpack and expand on that.

The core of the story, as I see it, is the aspect of your book that, if you take it away, your book would fall apart. Maybe it's the relationship between the sisters in your story. Maybe it's the futuristic world. Perhaps it's the sense of longing that permeates the whole book.

For an example from published literature, let's take *Charlotte's Web*, by E.B. White. The core of that story is the friendship between Wilbur the pig and Charlotte the spider. If you take that friendship away, you don't have a story—you have bacon (thank you, I'll be here all week).

Sometimes, you know what the core of your story is before you set a word on a page. Other times, it can take several drafts before you figure it out. For me, it varies from book to book. When I was writing my novel *Lights, Camera, Disaster*, I had no idea what the core of my story was—and it showed. The draft I sent in to my editor was about a girl whose English project video goes viral. My editor sent me a lovely, insightful, revision letter, asking that I "recalibrate" pages 160-230 to better reflect fame, which was the theme of the story.

As soon as I read that line, I realized that my book was not about fame at all. I was actually writing about creativity, and how sometimes creative kids don't fit in the expected boxes of success. It just *looked* like fame on the outside.

I "recalibrated" the book to reflect the core of the story—rewriting pages 160-230 and pages 1-159—taking out the viral video, and returning the manuscript with a cheerful note that read "Although you thought you were buying a book about fame, I was actually writing about creativity! I hope you like this version!"

Cores can be messy.

If you're having trouble identifying the core in your story, think about the element that, if your critique group told you to remove it, would cause you to clutch your pearls and gasp in horror. *"Remove the alien biker gang?! NEVER!!"* Chances are, there are only one or two things in your book that would cause you to have that reaction. Figure out what that element is and examine it. Why is this element so sacred to you? What aspects of the book rest on it? (An aside: If you have that pearl-clutching reaction to anything you are asked to change, you are likely not ready for feedback on that project yet. Put the book away and work on something else for a bit to give yourself the distance you need.)

Once you've identified the core of your particular story, you can work with it. If you know it while you're drafting, it can help you figure out where your manuscript is going to end. It can also help you identify steps in plot or character arc. Once I figure out what my core is, I write it on a sticky note and stick it to my laptop, so I don't lose track of it.

In revision, the core helps you separate the wheat from the chaff—or the relevant scenes from the irrelevant, as the case may be. Knowing your core can allow you to quickly look at a scene and assess it: Is this scene helping the book move toward the core of the story? How is it reflective of the core? For example, if the core of your book is about friendship, scenes where readers experience friendships forming move toward the core. Scenes where a friendship is tested or fractured also serve the core of the story—revealing to the main character how significant that friendship is. If there is a large swath of the book where friendship doesn't come up (the main character travels and is out of touch with a friend, and no longer thinks about that person), perhaps that section is not necessary, or needs to be "recalibrated" to better reflect the elements of friendship in the manuscript.

Figuring out the core requires us to think deeply about the story we're telling and what we're interested in exploring. It requires us to look beyond plot and character to the essence of our books. And as I said, it can be messy and hard. It takes time. Sometimes I need to talk about my book with a friend or critique partner to figure out where my core lies; other times, it's right there from the beginning.

All of this is to say, if the idea of a story's core is something that resonates with you, perhaps it will be as helpful for you as it is for me...and hopefully you'll figure it out before you have to "recalibrate" pages 160-230!

CHAPTER 7

GO FORWARD

I'm going to repeat myself in this collection, particularly about this: Writing is a process, and you have to figure out what your craft process is.

Practicing your craft is what makes you a writer.

One of the craft pieces that I've figured out is the value in always moving forward.

Stories have their own shapes, and in order to figure out that shape, I require a draft in front of me. Seeing that shape is what helps me decide what the book needs in revision, where I'm trying to go, and how I want to get there. It does me no good to rework a section until it's perfect before moving ahead, because the story shape is likely to change, and that section that I just perfected may not make the cut.

I have writer friends who are the exact opposite of me. Usually, they plan and plot a little more than I do, and they work out a lot more of their story before they sit down to write. Maybe that's you, too. And that's totally okay.

What works for me, however, is accumulating the words—the rough story. The book doesn't actually exist for me until it's on paper, and then I can start to move elements around and figure out what the story needs.

There's another reason why I want to suggest that you push forward: Fear.

Our writing exposes us, makes us vulnerable. It's hard to put yourself on the page, let alone share your thoughts and stories with the world. Fear is real, and it sets traps for creative people. One of the fear traps is perfection: Tinkering with something over and over until you get it exactly the way you want it is a protection from that vulnerability.

I'm not suggesting that we send our work out into the world before it's ready, but if you work on chapter one for months and years, or can't get to the middle because the beginning isn't perfect yet, it may not be the writing that's not working. You may be afraid.

This is what we know: Drafts are sucky and messy. They are filled with plot holes and dead ends, populated by flat characters and dumb story elements. Perhaps the setting is indistinct, and the dialogue sounds as wooden as a toy soldier. You know what? *That's okay.* Get it on the page, then go back and fix it later.

Worried that you'll forget to fix it? Leave yourself a note in the margin or at the end of the chapter of things you want to change or address. Get that worry out of your head and go forward. Keep writing. Push through.

There are two other reasons why pushing through is important:

1. Moving forward in the story teaches you how to move forward in the story. You'll never learn how to write the middle of the book if you never write a middle of a book.

2. You'll be a more experienced writer by the virtue of moving through the story. You're not the same writer at the end of a book that you were at the beginning. How can you be? You just wrote a whole entire book in between! (Go you!)

Pushing through to the end of my drafts means I have a complete book to revise—and that can sound intimidating to many people. But there's value in having the entire book together: You can see how things at the beginning can echo in the end, or how those pieces you struggled with fit together.

And I don't *just* push forward. At the beginning of most of my writing sessions, I go back about three to five pages, read them, and make small changes. This helps me immerse myself in the story before I tackle something new. If I discover a big change that I need to make—'eliminate the brother', 'add a biker gang'—I make a note of it and go forward with that piece adjusted. So if the brother exists in chapters one through four, and I decide to get rid of him, I make a note, and he doesn't appear in chapter five. Then I'll go back and take him out of the beginning later—during revision.

The only way we can write a book is by writing: one word at a time, marching across the blank page, adding up row by row. Right now, as I write these essays, that's exactly what I'm doing.

Today, it's a week before Christmas 2020. I'm writing one or two of these a day, aiming to be finished shortly after New Year's. I am not polishing each one to perfection, just getting them on the page. Once I have a bunch (there are nine right now), I'll send a stack to my critique group for their feedback. But I won't revise them until I've decided I'm done, because that's when I'll have a book.

Writing this book is scarier than my other projects, because I've never tackled nonfiction like this before. I'm also finding it exhilarating and fun. For now, I'm letting Exhilarating and Fun drive the bus, and Fear is a passenger in the middle row. We're getting to our destination together, whether Fear likes it or not.

Buckle Fear into its car seat and go. See where you end up.

CHAPTER 8

YOUR SAGGY MIDDLE

I DIDN'T WANT TO WRITE THIS ESSAY, SO I SKIPPED IT WHEN I wrote the first draft of this collection. Then I met with my critique group.

"You have to write about the middle," they said. "Everyone hates the middle," they said.

So do I, I thought.

"You need an essay about the middle," they said.

"Fine," I answered begrudgingly.

So, here we are. You've gotten excited and brainstormed in your notebook, developed your characters, figured out your plot, and started with a strong beginning. You're clipping along, writing, writing, writing, and then...

It comes to a screeching halt. Or the spigot slows to a slow drip instead of a steady stream.

It happens to all of us. The rosy glow of starting something new wears off. Your characters are casting about for stuff to do. You've identified problems within your story that you know you're going to have to go back and fix. You've been at this project for months—maybe years—and the words are not coming as smoothly. It's boring. It's hard. You feel whiny and petulant.

Congratulations! You've hit The Saggy Middle.

This is the point when we run out of the energy that gets us into a new project, but we haven't yet tapped into the energy that builds when we can see the end ahead. This feeling doesn't always come exactly at the middle of the book, but it's fairly close. Getting the story down on paper becomes *work*, not fun. Honestly, this is where a lot of people give up. They walk away from their book because they think something is wrong with them, or it, and it's not worth it to finish. What they don't understand is that *this is normal*. It's a regular part of the drafting process that almost every author must confront, at one point or another. Expecting it, recognizing it, and coming to terms with it is are other elements to include in our toolboxes.

I wish I could say, "Here are three things that you need to do, and you'll never deal with a Saggy Middle." I can't. If you're like most writers (myself included), you'll confront this with every book you write.

There are ways to navigate this path, but ultimately, you have to write through it. Here's how to make the road a little smoother:

Go back to your notebook. Now is a good time to remind yourself why you love your book. Read through the brainstorming pages from early in the process. What got you excited back then? What potential does your story have? Remind yourself. Sometimes, rereading these pages is enough to give me the bounce to move through this flabby, saggy stretch and get to the momentum of the ending.

Write your book a love note. Set pen to paper or fingers to keyboard and jot down all of the things you love about your story. What are you excited to reveal at the end? What readers will be affected by this book? What moments make you laugh, or cry, or keep you on the edge of your seat? Re-cultivating that rosy glow makes it easier to slog through this part of the story.

Skip it. As someone who primarily writes straight through the manuscript, this is hard for me. But sometimes, you need to just skip over the part that is sucking the enthusiasm out of you and move to a part you are excited to write. You can always go back. Or, maybe your book doesn't need the scene or section the way you'd conceived of it, and you can put something new in its place.

Practice acceptance. This is my preferred method. After writing eleven novels, I've come to recognize the Saggy Middle as, well, not exactly an old friend, but more of an annoying unwelcome houseguest. "Oh. You again," is my approach. I acknowledge that they've settled on my couch for the time being, and since they've been here before, I know I'll find a way to send them on their way. Eventually.

Write hot garbage. Scenes with no arc, big brackets [insert really meaningful conversation here], a list of stuff that you *think* should happen but aren't all that excited to write...just get it on paper. This works well if you're like me, and you are loathe to skip sections. I'll write some hot garbage that I can fix later, and just get through this part of the draft.

Reward yourself. Now is the time to really lean into making writing enjoyable. I will talk a little more about this later on, but treat yourself during a writing session: music you like, a beverage you enjoy, anything that makes you want to sit down and work can be quite helpful during this stage.

THERE ARE no shortcuts to writing; no magic. Getting through the middle means...getting through the middle. But knowing that it's coming and not being discouraged or panicked at how you feel when you get there will hopefully make it a little easier.

CHAPTER 9

PLOT IS FOR DEAD PEOPLE, PORE-FACE

LORRIE MOORE HAS A SHORT STORY TITLED "How to Become A Writer," which is a second-person homage to the winding path that we take to following our passion. One of the sections in the piece has the narrator turning in a story that they've written for a class, and the teacher responds that they have no sense of plot. Moore's narrator goes home to "faintly scrawl in pencil beneath his black-lined comments, "Plots are for dead people, pore-face."

That line cracks me up.

I am a character-based writer. Almost all of my stories begin with a character, and I then figure out what is going to happen to them. Plot and narrative arc have always been a struggle for me, and although I've gotten better at them over time, I've certainly hissed that line at my manuscripts more than once.

Plot is the movement of the story; it's what happens in the story world to send our characters on their emotional journey and (hopefully) help them change. Our characters change due to their experiences via the plot.

I used to characterize myself as a *pantser*. I'd start with my character, do a ton of brainstorming around who they were, start drafting, and try to figure out the plot as I went along. A lot of writers do this. It takes time, and it brought me to a ton of dead ends. I'd try something out, backtrack—deleting entire sections—go in another direction, try something else. It wasted my time and energy, neither of which I have oodles to spare.

But I didn't know how to handle plot any other way. Writing an outline seemed to suck the life out of the book (why write the story, when I'd already figured out what was going to happen?). Discovery is part of my process.

I was stuck.

I wrote three novels like this, fumbling around and figuring it out as I went (four, if you count the one I never published). This meant I wrote the first fifty pages of *The Total Tragedy of a Girl Named Hamlet* five times. That's a whole book's worth of rewriting, just to get that story off the ground! When I worked on *Notes from an Accidental Band Geek*, I ended up removing an entire plot thread because I couldn't articulate why I needed it to my editor—and now I know that was the wrong decision. That book is lesser because I didn't understand how that plot worked on more than just an intuitive level.

For my fourth novel, *Moxie and the Art of Rule Breaking*, I tackled a mystery based on a real-life art heist. It took about thirty seconds for me to realize that I couldn't fumble my way through this. Mysteries have a tight structure. I needed a villain, clues, a mystery to solve, red herrings, etc. My "write it until you get it right" approach wasn't going to cut it. Plus, I was pregnant, and the book and baby were due awfully close together.

There had to be a better way.

I needed to plan.

At that point, I grabbed some big paper and worked backwards —figuring out where (literally) I wanted the story to end and jotting notes here and there about the moments that would take me to that point. Instead of an outline, which felt rigid to me, I had a path of stepping stones through the book. It was loose enough to give me plenty to discover, but I had a sense of where the story was going and what I had to include. And it worked: *Moxie* was nominated for an Edgar Award in the Juvenile Fiction category by the Mystery Writers of America and ended up being one of four finalists in 2014.

Maybe plots weren't for dead people.

Since writing *Moxie*, I've spent more time learning about how plot works. I've studied screenwriting pretty intensely for the past four years, examining how writers fashion compelling stories into the limited space of a script. Blake Snyder's *Save the Cat* is a favorite craft book of mine, and I now use his Beat Sheet to plan out the plots of my stories before I write—and I "reverse engineer" my books after drafting them, plugging what actually has happened back into the Beat Sheet to see if my story works. It's made a tremendous difference in my writing.

The Beat Sheet identifies about fifteen plot points that help guide the main character through their story. Some of it parallels the hero's journey. All of it was taken from a deep study of commercially successful films (so it's more applicable if you're writing a commercially-themed book). It gave me the clearest way to articulate how the elements of my story worked together and built upon one another to get to the conclusion.

Save the Cat and the Beat Sheet aren't the only plot helpers out there. You can check out Dan Harmon's Story Circles, the Snowflake Method, the structure of folktales and fairy tales. Grabbing some of your favorite books, or books that you want to emulate in your writing, and mapping out how the plot unfolds in those stories is another way to identify what plot structure works for you. Lastly, a simple Google search of "plot structure examples" opens a whole rabbit hole to explore.

Maybe you love plot, and that's the thing that comes easiest for you. Maybe, like me, you think it's for dead people. Plot *is* story, though. And stories have specific mechanisms that make them work for our readers. Our characters need to struggle, to make bad choices and learn from their mistakes. They need to cause things to happen, so they have regret and make changes. The Beat Sheet reminds me of this and allows me the room to still have the thrill of discovering surprising moments in my characters' journeys.

Are you a pantser who struggles with plot? Or a rigid outliner who plots every moment before you sit down to begin? Either way is fine, as long as they are working for you. But if they're not working, or if you're an in-betweener, like me, forge your own path and see what unlocks the element of plot for you.

CHAPTER 10

(DON'T) MAKE IT UP: TURNING FACT INTO FICTION

ONE OF THE MOST SEARING MEMORIES I HAVE AS A WRITER is from a short story workshop I took as an undergrad. It was one of the few creative writing courses that my English major track allowed me to take, and I was elated to be in the class. I'd written a story based on a terrible date I'd been on. I'd submitted it for workshop, sure that I was going to receive glowing feedback and that my professor would pull me aside and hand me a one-way ticket to New York's publishing elite.

Instead, my professor shook her head. And frowned.

"It's cartoonish," she said. "It doesn't feel authentic. It doesn't go anywhere."

"It really happened," I said, my voice barely above a whisper, gutted.

"Real life does not translate well to fiction," she said. She went on, but I sunk in my seat, hurt and vulnerable.

It *had* happened—all of it. I'd changed the characters in the story (a little), but they were real people. When I recounted the story of the date to friends, it always got a big laugh. I sulked, fuming a little bit at my professor and deciding that if I had been able to execute it better on the page, I'd have received a better reaction. It was my writing that was terrible, I decided.

As I progressed in my writing journey, I've come back to this moment a lot. What I didn't understand, and what I think I missed when I retreated to lick my wounds, was a crucial lesson about writing from real life.

Real life frequently does not work when we turn it in to fiction. Fictional stories have a shape and theme and purpose that our bumbling, awkward real-life lives often lack. It's part of the reason why we love stories so much—they are elegant. Characters grow and change in these packages of experience. Most of the time, in our own lives, growth is ugly and slow and painful—and it takes a really long time. But in between the pages of a novel? Characters bloom.

This doesn't mean we can't use our real-life experiences in our fiction. I used a lot of true anecdotes and experiences in *Notes from an Accidental Band Geek*, because I spent eight years performing in marching bands and wanted to capture some of those big moments in that book. In order to do that, though, I had to unhook those experiences and stories from my life, and give them to my character in a way that was authentic and made sense in the manuscript. *I was willing to change the truth of my experience in order to fit the truth of the story*—which is something I didn't do in that awful date story in college.

Where lived experience and truth come into play in all of our fiction is via character emotions. The feelings we've had in response to events in our lives are ripe for mining. We can transcribe those exact emotions as we felt them. Betrayal, loss, joy, fear, anger, frustration...think back to when you felt those big feelings. What was going on in your body? In your mind? The more specific we can be in recording how we felt, the more authentic our characters' emotional reactions will be in that moment in the story.

For example, your character may feel deeply betrayed by her best friend. You can go to a time in your life when you felt that same level of betrayal—and maybe it wasn't a friend who hurt you, but a boss, spouse, coworker, or family member—and document that emotional reaction and then give it to your character. The aching heart, the hitch in breathing, the weak knees...all of those elements will ring true to your reader, because they came from your true experience.

This method of using emotional truth is much more effective than trying to take that funny story or sad story that happened to you and transcribe it as it happened on the page. The results are almost always far clumsier and have less grace than the rest of our writing does. Ironically, the more we unhook our experiences from ourselves and get more specific with our characters, the better our books become.

That's the truth.

CHAPTER 11

SPRINKLE, DON'T POUR: GETTING THE DETAILS RIGHT

ONE OF THE PHRASES THAT I FIND MYSELF REPEATING TO my students (and myself) over and over again is, "sprinkle, don't pour." This bit of wisdom is applicable to decorating baked goods, spicing up soups and stews, and improving any piece of writing.

When I'm drafting, even if I've done a lot of prewriting and planning, I'm still discovering details about the story and its characters as I go. I'm teaching myself about the world of the story, the characters, their goals and dreams, etc.

And then I figure something—or someone—out, get really excited, and put what I know into the piece. Sometimes all of it at once. These are what we refer to as info dumps. Long descriptions, worldbuilding, character traits, recounting conversations to catch the reader up on what's happened...info dumps, all of it.

When I'm going through my draft, I look for those clumps of info—those info dumps—and break the clumps up, distributing that material throughout the text. Modern audiences don't have the attention span to sit through long, detailed descriptions. And sometimes, that material is only there for me as the author. In that case, it needs to be completely removed.

Most of the time, however, those clumps of text can be threaded through other parts of the story. Do we need the whole description of the main character's bedroom right now? Or do we just need the part about her favorite stuffed animal and her blue comforter because she's super upset and needs something to snuggle? Our character isn't paying attention to the *Frozen: The Musical* poster on her wall right now, and neither should our reader. We should keep the character's (and the reader's) focus on what is critical in the moment.

This applies to character details, setting details, backstory... putting in too much all at once will actually water down the information you're trying to convey. People can only hold so much info in their brains, and if you front-load it all, they aren't going to remember it thirty, forty, or a hundred pages later.

Instead, we need to do what Alisha Niehaus, the editor for my debut novel, *Models Don't Eat Chocolate Cookies*, told me, with regard to minor characters: "Every time someone comes on stage, we should learn something new about them." It applies to character and everything other element, as well. We need to gradually add those world building, backstory, and setting details to our manuscripts. Our readers' brains build a picture as the story unfolds, and each new piece of information contributes a piece of that image.

Tantalize your readers by evenly doling out the details and descriptions, and you'll give them a deliciously rich reading experience to savor.

CHAPTER 12

ARE WE THERE YET?

Think about it: have you ever raced up to someone and said, "The beginning of this book is so amazing! You will love it!!"?

You have not.

Beginnings get an awful lot of attention in craft discussions, but when it comes to what readers remember and appreciate about a book, endings get the spotlight. Endings stay with readers. They are literally the last element in the book, and so they are the final connection that our readers have with our story. A critical question for me is, *how do I want my reader to feel once they put the book down?* Ultimately, I want them to be satisfied, but satisfaction comes in many forms.

━━━

I Can Get Some Satisfaction

Endings tie our stories together and fulfill what we set out to do in the beginning of the manuscript. Remember when we talked about The Promise at the beginning of our book? Our ending has to deliver on that promise. If we promised a magical romance, those two characters should either end up together, or the reader should have a strong intimation that they *will* end up together. And there'd better be magic. If we promised a mystery, we want our readers to have experienced the search for clues, some danger, red herrings...all of the items that make up the elements in a mystery novel. Fulfilling The Promise that we make at the beginning of our novels is key to earning reader satisfaction.

Satisfaction doesn't mean "perfectly wrapped up," however. There's ample room for ambiguity. In fact, an ambiguous ending can be just as satisfying as one that is more tightly wrapped up, if done well.

Effective ambiguous endings revolve around what the reader understands about the character. If authors address where the character is now in their journey and if they changed, readers are more tolerant of a less clear-cut ending. Other important questions that writers need to address revolve around their characters' *capacity* for change: Did they change? *Can* they? What is their hope for the future?

It's important to acknowledge that different genres of books have different rules (I hate that word) around endings. For example, in a traditional romance novel, the couple needs to get together by the end of the book otherwise, the audience's expectation won't be met, and the readership will be incredibly frustrated—which is the exact opposite of how we want readers to feel at the end of the story. In children's books, where I'm most comfortable, there's almost always a glimmer of hope at the end of the story. No matter how dark your young adult novel gets, that readership needs—and expects—that spark of light at the end of the book. Perhaps that main character is still in the same situation, but what she's learned from her journey are the skills that let us, the readers, know that she will handle things differently going forward. A glimmer of hopefulness is critical for this market.

Adult literary fiction has more leeway with regard to endings. Plenty of adult literary novels have bleak endings where the main characters don't change or have changed very little. Many have dark endings with no hope. If that's the category in which you're writing, you have that option at your disposal. The way you figure out what the rules are in your genre is to simply read a lot in the genre in which you are writing, and pay attention to how those endings work.

EMOTIONAL DEVASTATION

Beyond satisfaction, there are other emotions that our readers can feel around the endings of our books. I always try to figure out how I want my reader to feel at the end of my manuscript when I'm doing my prewriting. Is the reader going to cheer for the main character? Do I want readers to feel proud, or determined? Maybe they'll feel sad, but with a bit of that watery smile on their face, knowing that the character is going to be okay? Figuring this out before I start to write my book helps me build a story towards that emotional ending. The actual ending can—and does often—change, but the important thing is I have an idea of where I'm going when I begin. It's like driving to the store: when I get there, I may end up in a different parking *space* than I intended, but I bring the story to the same parking *lot*.

I asked a friend about the ending she was crafting for her most recent project. "How do you want your reader to feel when you're done?" I said.

"Emotionally devastated," was her reply.

Well okay then.

Once we know how we want the reader to feel, we can work to ensure we stick the landing in our drafts and revisions.

An Aside: Many Endings, One Story

I do need to point out that there are lots of endings in your novel: scene endings, chapter endings, section endings. We need to address all of them, because they each have a purpose in your story.

Scene endings transition us from one moment or section of story to the next. In revision, assess what the purpose of that scene is and whether it's been achieved by the end of the scene. For example, if the scene's purpose was to give your character new information, do they have it by the end of the scene? If you can't identify what the purpose of the scene is, you need to either change the scene or cut it.

Chapter endings move us through a larger section of text or provide an opportunity to switch points of view, depending on the type of book you're writing. Chapter endings can be natural stopping points for readers—a good place to put that bookmark and go do something else. Do you want that? Or do you want your chapter endings to be emotional or action-oriented cliffhangers that pull the reader through to the next chapter and make it impossible to put the book down? You may want a mix of both.

Lastly, section endings are also significant. Not every book is broken up into sections, but if yours is—why? What is different about your sections that warrants that grouping over—or in addition to—chapters? Once you identify the purpose of breaking the book into sections, you'll be able to decide on the most effective ending. Perhaps there is a big time jump between the sections, or perhaps there are different narrators for each, or perhaps they mark different stages in the character's development—you get to choose, but you need to know your rationale. This will enable you to write that section ending effectively.

How You End It

Different types of books have different endings, and we need to understand how those work.

Stand-alone Novels. Stand-alones are stories where the story is contained to one volume; they aren't a series. This is the only experience your readers will have with these characters, so we want to leave this world and these people in a memorable way. We can add an emotional punch at the end, and we want our readers to be satisfied. The big don't for stand-alones: ending on a cliffhanger. Ambiguity is okay, but an unresolved cliffhanger is a recipe for disaster at the end of a stand-alone.

Big Bows. Some stand-alones wrap up their endings in a big bow. Every last detail is addressed, and this can be very satisfying for certain types of readers. Most romance novels end with a big bow, and that is what expected for the genre. Mysteries can also end this way—if our detective solves the case, catches the culprit, and understands the motive, that's a big ole' bow, right there.

In children's books, big bow endings can be found in middle grade novels (readers aged nine and up) and chapter books (readers aged six-eight). These emerging readers want to know what happens to the characters and need to feel okay about leaving that world.

Loose Ends/Ambiguous. Ambiguous endings can also be really effective, but they work best when our readers have a solid understanding of either plot or character. If our reader understands our character's goals and how they've grown over the course of the story, but doesn't exactly know every little thing that happens at the end, the reader can project a path that the character might take. Our reader feels good about where the character is going, even though pieces of the plot may be unresolved.

If the narrator is unreliable—or readers don't know as much about them as they'd like, but do understand how the plot works—ambiguity can be effective. For example, perhaps there's an impending event at the end of your story—a wedding —and your main character is a bridesmaid. Readers may not know what choice the bridesmaid is going to make, but we can project that the wedding will happen and see a scenario for the main character.

Ambiguous endings work well for novels geared toward adult audiences and young adult readers.

Series. Series are a whole different animal, especially if you're pre-published. For novels that are the first and middle of the series, thinking about your endings as a double rainbow can be helpful. Here's what I mean: A double-rainbow story arc has two arcs, one that wraps up in the first book to keep readers satisfied, but also a second arc that carries over into other aspects of the next book. Lots of times, publishers hesitate to purchase all of the books in a series out of the gate, and so your book needs to feel like it could end with book one (in case it doesn't sell well, and your publisher doesn't want to put out the rest), but leave open the possibility of more to come. For example, perhaps your main character has been on a quest in book one. By the end, they complete their quest, but along the way discover that they have a sibling they never knew about. Readers are satisfied by the end of the quest, but see an opportunity for book two to revolve around the sibling.

The last book in the series is critical. How do you want to leave readers feeling after they have invested all this time into your books? Look at two of the biggest franchises in young adult publishing: Stephenie Meyer wrapped up *Twilight* with a big bow. Bella gets everything she wants, with no risk and no loss. This approach can be risky as an author. Our readers know that life is frequently messy, and we don't get everything we want. In *Harry Potter*, Rowling ensures that Harry gets what he has wanted—a family—but he suffers loss and sacrifices a lot throughout both that last book and the entire series. As a reader, we see our human experience reflected in those books, and they feel more complete.

———

Are We There Yet?

Endings are super important to our work and can feel really hard to get right. In order to nail them, we need to look at the book we're writing and ask ourselves:

- Did I fulfill the promise I made at the beginning of the story?
- Who has power at the end of my story? Hopefully your main character, but maybe not. If not, *why* not?
- Is the most powerful person featured at the end?
- What are the last words of spoken dialogue in the book? Who says them? Why?
- Does the book end with dialogue or with narrative description? Which one is more powerful in your story?

———

UNDERSTANDING the emotional tone you're going for will make the book a success for you—and your reader. When in doubt, write a little further, or go back and look for a natural ending earlier in the last chapter.

THE END
(Of this section, anyway)

REVISION

CHAPTER 13

EVERYTHING SUCKS--AND THAT'S OKAY

This piece is about how your writing sucks. And that's okay.

Everyone's writing sucks at first. Seriously.

The best thing we can do for ourselves as writers is accept the fact, early on, that our drafts are not the soaring, gilded-winged birds that we envision in our heads. They are awkward, misshapen dodos that flap about and screech, dragging one broken wing across the page and making us feel like we'll never get this right (or perhaps your drafts *are* gorgeous creatures, in which case you don't need this book, and we won't be friends).

Here's the thing: embracing the suckiness of our drafts gives us freedom to make them better. There's no expectation that those drafts are going to be good, let alone great—we just have to get the words on the page. To me, that freedom from perfection is such a relief.

It doesn't have to be good, it just has to get done.

That is the mantra I'm using as I write this collection. I'm writing one to two pieces a day, at the holidays, during a pandemic. It's fine. These are *not* great right now. And that's totally okay! I don't expect them to be great. I just want them written, so that I can work to make them better.

If you never write it, you can't work with it. Thinking about your story, wishing it were done, castigating yourself because it's not going to be as good as you want it to be, so why bother writing it...*none* of that actually gets the words on the page.

What does get words on the page? Sitting and typing them (or using speech recognition software and talking your book through, or writing longhand if that's your jam). There are only methods, no shortcuts.

I'll say it again: There are no shortcuts.

This brings me back to messy manuscripts: It's okay. I'll write a paragraph, then highlight it and leave myself a note in the margin: Make better. And then I'll move on.

Sometimes, I get to a place where I know I need to add a joke, but I'm not feeling particularly funny. I put some square brackets [like these] and write [insert joke here] in them. Or [insert funny scene with the cow]. Or whatever. And I keep going.

Some days, I agonize over those scenes, because I feel up to writing them. But if I don't, I can move on.

My first drafts have flat characters, weak plot arcs, cliches, and holes you can drive a truck through. That's fine! The shape is there, there are words on the page, and I can work with that.

Part of the reason we think our work should be better than it is when we draft is because we are always comparing our drafts to other people's finished products. I'll say it again: *We compare our drafts to others' finished products.* The bound book you are holding in your hand or reading on your device went through a lot of steps before it got to you. It did not unfold majestically from the author's head in the state it is in right now (if it did, we are not friends with that person). The author drafted it, perhaps a critique group or partner read it, their agent and editor reviewed it—usually more than once—a copyeditor fixed all of the grammatical mistakes, and there's another round of last-minute edits once it is in layouts and before it goes to production. That's six sets of eyes on it, minimum, before yours hit it.

Comparing your draft to another author's finished product is akin to seeing a supermodel in a magazine and wishing you could look like them. They have a trainer, a chef, a strict regime they follow, a beauty staff at their disposal for hair and makeup tips, and exceptional lighting. Likely a big fan to blow their hair around, too. Then comes the airbrushing and Photoshop. Sure, maybe you'd *like* to look like that, but it's super hard with most people's resources.

When it comes to our writing, though, we *can* put it through its paces and bring it from drab to fab, no hair and makeup needed. We just have to be willing to put in the time and not let our disappointment at its suckiness derail us. To use a different analogy, a first draft is like getting the ingredients for dinner out of the cabinet and putting them on the counter. The dried pasta, tomatoes, olive oil, and assorted spices are what you need for the meal, but there's a bunch of steps between taking the stuff out of the cabinet and getting it plated and ready to enjoy. Our first drafts are the ingredients on the counter. We have to collect everything we need before we can start, and then the dish gets better and better as we add the next element.

Be proud of your sucky drafts, because you wrote them. You'll be able to fix them, and the final product will be delicious—and beautiful.

CHAPTER 14

THE ART OF GIVING CRITIQUE

I HAD AN EPIPHANY IN MY DAUGHTER'S SECOND GRADE classroom. Her class was doing a "writer's workshop" event, and parents were invited to observe the process. The kids took their stories from station to station around the room, reading their work aloud and getting feedback on it. The teacher explained what was going to happen at each station. "This," she said, with a grand gesture, "is the Feedback Station. You'll read your story, then listen quietly while your audience tells you what they like and maybe what you need to change."

She went on, but my brain went elsewhere.

In that moment, I realized that the way I'd talked about critique —the way I'd taught critiquing—was wrong. It wasn't actually the way any authors whom I know worked, and *it wasn't the way I worked with my own critique group.*

I'm sure the stories I heard that day were adorable, but I couldn't stop thinking about the drastically wrong way we talk about giving feedback. I feel like I need to apologize to a decade of students and adult learners, because this is not how true critique works at all.

Sitting and absorbing a free-for-all of comments is actually ineffective and can be damaging. Writing *requires* feedback, criticism, and changes. It's how our stories get better and how we grow as writers. It's part of being a professional writer: Agents, editors, and readers will offer their advice and suggestions to make your book better. This is part of what we *do*.

But it can also be incredibly damaging if done incorrectly. Receiving—and giving—critique is a skill that needs to be consciously worked on and developed as we go through our writing journey.

The epiphany that zinged me like a bold of lightning was about the "sit silently and listen to the feedback." There is no time in my writing life where I hand over a manuscript, tell people to "have at it," and sit back, waiting, docilely accepting whatever it is that people want to say about my manuscript.

Instead, I typically hand over my manuscript with a note to my group members, saying, "This is what I'm working on. Can you give your attention to A, B, and C? Also, I'm struggling with X." This information gives my readers direction in where to place their attention, and it ensures that I get the feedback I'm looking for on the parts of the book with which I'm struggling. This is not to say that my group members won't also offer advice on items that were not on my list—of course they do!— but by telling them where to focus, I end up getting exactly what I need, and then some.

We know where in our work we are having a hard time. We know where we are struggling. We should specifically ask for help in those areas, to ensure we get what we need.

As I've applied this idea to my own work and my classroom critiques, I ask students to place a note at the top of their submissions for critique. The note asks for four pieces of information:

1. Where are you in your process? A first draft is different than an eighth revision, which is different than copyedits. By understanding where our writer is in their process, we can tailor our comments more effectively. For example, an in-process first draft may likely involve exploration and have more continuity errors. I can overlook those to focus on helping the writer complete that manuscript. They don't need me to dissect their piece—it could cause them to lose momentum and not finish their book. Conversely, someone who is deep into a revision will need more intense scrutiny to ensure their book is holding together and communicating its story well.

2. What are you doing well? Although it may be difficult for some of us to actually admit out loud that we are doing something right, we know what we are doing well when we're writing. For example, as I draft this book, I know that my content is solid—so I'll tell my critique group that I believe this book offers good information (they will let me know if they disagree). Knowing what someone believes they are doing well is critical to this stage of the process. If someone says they feel their dialogue kicks butt, and I read it and it is flat and stilted, I'll know to tread lightly and be extra careful with my word choice. This does not mean dialogue is off-limits for critiquing;

it means I have to be more empathetic when criticizing it. I might say something like, "You felt your dialogue is really strong here, but I'm seeing a few places where it's not working for me. Perhaps go back and look at page X, where I feel the dialogue isn't working as well."

3. What are you struggling with? Writers are super good at this part. We can give you a laundry list of things we are sucking at—plot, motivation, voice, setting—and knowing where my critique partner is struggling homes in my reading and critical analysis of that element. If plot is the source of their problem, I'm going to read carefully and think about how the plot is working. Where is it hanging together? Where is it falling apart? What holes can I identify? All of this will help me offer solutions that the writer can use.

4. What do you want me to focus on? The answer might be a specific page, chapter, section, or element. It could be anything. But whatever it is, I can point my attention at it and hopefully give my partner the suggestions and help they need, or reassurance that the biker gang scene is working well, and they can move on.

Once you have this information, you can then address the method of giving critique. Typically, I read through a selection once without making any suggestions—noting, perhaps, where I get bored or lost, but not writing anything down. During my second read-through, I start looking at it more closely, jotting down comments and adding suggestions where appropriate. Next, I organize my response. Some members of our critique group will organize their responses by craft element (plot, character, etc.); others use a list approach of what is working well, what isn't clear, and where they have questions. There are all kinds of ways to structure the feedback, but it's important that you organize your ideas. You want to be able to effectively communicate them to the author. Lastly, don't forget to point out and acknowledge the parts of the manuscript that you like.

The goal in giving a good critique is to be honest and to help your partner tell their story in the most clear and effective way possible. Be mindful of your partner's goals with this piece: Will they be seeking publication with it? Querying an agent? Using it for a contest entry? Presenting it to their close families as a gift? This is not about what we want to do with their story; it's about helping *them* do what they want with it.

Giving a constructive, thoughtful critique will help them do just that.

CHAPTER 15

HOW TO RECEIVE CRITIQUE

I've seen it happen: A casually tossed-off comment from a well-meaning critique group member, and the writer's eyes dull, head droops, pen stops taking notes.

Receiving critique is hard. Having someone else tell us that something isn't working in the book that we spent months to create stings. And depending on where we are in our process, getting a critique at the wrong time, or in the wrong way, can derail us or even cause us to roll up our work. This is why we need to be clear in our needs (see "The Art of Giving Critique"), and we need to have a plan to deal with the critique we receive.

As I mentioned in the other essay, part of being a writer is sharing our work, and that means we are going to receive feedback on it. Editors, agents, and readers are all going to offer comments on our work during different stages of the writing process. We have to be able to navigate the comments we receive, process them, and know how to incorporate them into our manuscript.

Before we get to that point, however, we have to assess if we're even ready for feedback. Ask yourself these questions:

1. Am I ready for feedback? Did you just finish this chapter ten minutes ago? Did you type "the End" yesterday? Look, I know you're excited to ship that manuscript or those pages out to someone else, but you may need to give yourself some space from the writing before you solicit feedback—especially if you're dealing with a short turnaround between the time you send the selection to a critique partner and when you get the feedback. My group meets every two weeks. If I send them a couple of chapters, two weeks later I'll have six people's opinions on it (we usually take 6-8 weeks when we read a novel). So I may wait two weeks, send it, and then I'm getting a critique a month after I wrote it. It's less fresh and feels less raw this way.

2. Am I ready to make substantive changes? If you are still too close to your piece, you may not be ready to dive in and do a true revision or what needs to be done to bring your work to the next level. Again—time is a factor here. It's the best way to separate ourselves from our work and give us the distance we need to be objective about what's on the page.

3. Do I know the core of my story? Going into a critique, it's really helpful to know the core of your story. This is the thing that you know you're not going to change—it's what you're working to enhance and strengthen as you go through the editing process (see "The Core of the Story"). Sometimes, however, we don't know what our core is, or we're not sure.

When this happens to me (frequently), I use my critiques, listen carefully to what others say about my book, and figure out what resonates with me. I can use the critique to immediately realize what is and is not important to me, based on my reactions to ideas.

4. Am I willing to change anything to make the core stronger? Can I recognize what is detrimental to my core? Would you change a plot line? Take out a character? Cut the first fifty pages? You may need to, to get to the book you are trying to write. Are you ready to do that at this point? If not, take more time.

5. Who can help me see what needs to be worked on? My critique group members have a range of skills and expertise in giving feedback. I know I'm going to get a well-rounded review from the whole group. Sometimes, though, especially if I've done a few sets of revisions with them, I get to a point where I don't need the whole group's feedback—I just need one or two members to apply their skills to the book. Other times, I have to go outside of the group to get feedback from other readers. I may need a sensitivity reader if I'm writing a character from a perspective not my own. I may need an expert to review logistical or technical issues. Figuring out who those people are can take time, so use those connections you make as you network to help you bring your manuscript to the best critique readers possible.

6. Do I know what to do with the feedback I get? This is a key step that not everyone thinks about when receiving critique. Once you feel the feelings around the feedback, what are you going to do with that? Will you make a list to tackle by chapter? By element (plot, character, setting, etc)? How are you going to approach this step? I make handwritten notes in my project notebook every time I get a critique. When each person discusses the novel selection, I make a separate notebook entry. That way, I have the list of questions and concerns about the manuscript, and I also know who had those issues—so I can go back and ask clarifying questions at any point. Then, I gather all of the feedback and make a master list from which to work. Remember: You are the final arbiter of your story. You don't have to make any changes that don't make sense for your manuscript. But *do* carefully consider all feedback. Something that a critique partner brings up might not be the right solution for a problem, but they may have identified something in your story that needs fixing.

What Happens if It Goes Bad?

Being prepared and having a plan makes the revision process go along a lot more smoothly. But sometimes, critiques don't go well in the moment. I've been in critique sessions that go off the rails: People get caught up in a specific bit of minutia, or they argue about something, or—worst case scenario—someone is rude and dismissive of another writer's work.

This is where having rules about critiquing behavior and decorum is crucial, but sometimes it just goes bad. What to do?

1. You can stop it. We're long taught to be quiet and listen during critique sessions—but you don't have to sit there and do that. It's perfectly acceptable to put an end to the conversation and move on. Oftentimes, other members will feel awkward and upset as well but be unsure if they can stop this process.

You can. You should. And if it's not you being critiqued, speak up and support your fellow writer.

2. Prep language in advance. Some things you can say to get things back on track: "This is not helpful. Can we focus on X?" "I asked about X, not Y." "Okay...this is a good place to stop." If you have those phrases at the ready, you're more likely to use them.

3. Focus the critique. Go to the "Art of Giving Critique" in this book. Use the pre-critique set up questions to direct readers' attention and conversation.

4. Leave the group. If the group you're in is dysfunctional, if members don't treat one another's work with respect, if someone hogs the meeting or consistently doesn't come prepared....you don't have to stay. Bow out and find another group. It's not for you to fix it or stick it out to make it work. There are plenty of other writers out there who can help you make your stories soar.

REMEMBER: the purpose of critique is to make our work stronger, more clear, more exciting to our readers. It's not to tear down someone's effort—it's to constructively point out the spots where it can be improved. This is how our writing gets better. Planning, preparation, and giving our work some space and time before we send it out ensures that we're able to confidently take advantage of the gift of other people's investment in our writing.

CHAPTER 16

FEEDBACK: WHAT DO I DO WITH IT?

CONGRATULATIONS! YOU'VE SUCCESSFULLY NAVIGATED your critique group session, listened attentively as your critiquers gave you specific feedback and suggestions based on the info you've provided, and you've clarified any questions you have. You now have a big ole' list of stuff that you wrote down, a pile of scribbled-on manuscripts that your critique group members gave you, and an abiding sense of dread.

What do you *do* with this stuff? Where do you start?

This is one of those moments when having your toolbox handy can be really helpful.

First, feel the feels. At this stage, when I get feedback from my writing group, I'm able to dive right in—I have a long-standing relationship with them, and I'm used to our methods and approach. But when my editors send me an editorial letter, I need to take a little time with that. Sometimes it's a day or two; sometimes I'll circle that seven-page, single-spaced editorial letter like a wary cat, nibbling my way through a bag of Ghirardelli dark chocolate squares. Just as we need some objectivity to be ready to submit our manuscript for critique, we need to cultivate a little objectivity when working with our edits. It needs to feel a little less *close*, you know? So take a breath; take some space.

Accept that you need to do the work. My books are far from perfect. Yours are, too. That's okay. We talk about that in "Everything Sucks—and That's Okay". Remind yourself that doing the work is part of this. It's okay. The book is going to be even better when you're done. Hooray!

Organize the feedback. When you're able to look at your notes with a sense of expectation and curiosity, you're in the right headspace to dive in to that revision. Figure out which way makes sense for you to organize the items on which you have to work: By chapter? By element (plot, character, etc)? By smallest tweaks to largest changes? Whatever makes sense to you is fine. Sometimes I print the editorial letter and highlight the things I need to change, then check those items off as I complete each task. Typically, I make a master list, organized by plot element/character, and work that way. It depends on the book.

Assess the feedback. Go through the list carefully. Are there things that jump out at you right away as not making sense for this project? Things that take you away from the book you're trying to write? Cross them off the list. *You are not obligated to make every change every person suggests to you.* What you *are* obligated to do: See if the feedback you're eliminating is actually pointing out a problem. If it is, perhaps you need to solve it in a different way than was suggested. Or, perhaps you're not being clear, and your critique partner misinterpreted part of a scene that lead to an erroneous conclusion. In this case, their conclusion may be erroneous, but your lack of clarity led them down that road. Lastly, if the feedback is subjective and is not actually addressing an issue, ditch it. You can do that! Besides, you have plenty of other stuff to work on.

Prepare. Decide how you are going to do this work. I print out my manuscripts, three-hole-punch them, and put them in a binder. I print my revision list and put it in the front pocket. I then make my edits by hand on the document, then input them back into the document on the computer when I've completed the whole by-hand revision. Maybe you are going to copy your manuscript file and work directly on the computer. Whatever works for you, do it.

Begin. Dive in, be brave, and make those changes. Your book will be better for it!

A WORD OF CAUTION: Don't rush this process. Work your way through it, steadily or in fits and starts, but let it take the time it needs to take. This step is what elevates the craft of your manuscript. Give your art and creativity the time they need to truly bring this book to life.

And when you're done? Well, let it sit for a bit...and do it again.

CHAPTER 17

PUT THE OCTOPUS IN THE BOX: OBJECTIVITY & REVISION

I LIKE ANALOGIES, IF YOU HAVEN'T FIGURED THAT OUT already. One of my favorites involves one of my favorite aspects of the writing process: Revision. For me, revision is like putting an octopus in a box—when I get three tentacles in, four more shoot out and wave around. The fifth takes off my hat. I get six in, two more swing out. And so on.

Revision, though, is more problem solving than octopus wrangling. As much as drafting is an act of creativity, revision brings forth a different (perhaps less sexy?) element of the craft —but it's also a major act of creativity. It's the step(s) in the process that I love most of all, because it means I can shape the story into whatever final form it's going to take. I'd rather revise all day than draft.

In my teaching, I come across many writers who dread revision. Sometimes, they dread it because they've invested so much time into drafting that they don't want to change their words.

Sometimes, they don't like it because they find it overwhelming. Sometimes, it's because they don't know where to start.

Here's the thing: Revision is part of writing, and the more comfortable we get with it, the more our work will connect with readers. Revision makes our writing go from good to great, and from great to excellent.

The key to revision? Objectivity. When we cultivate objectivity, we are better able to see what's on the page and the value in making changes to allow our work to grow stronger. Remember, the goal of good writing is to connect with our reader. Revision makes our work clearer and that connection more effective. However, it can be hard to be objective about our own work, so this is a skill that we need to develop as we progress though our writing journey.

So how can we cultivate that objectivity and get the octopus in the box?

Take time. The more time we take away from our manuscript, the further away it feels. This makes it easier for us to separate ourselves from the act of writing it—from the time we've invested in crafting those words—and we become able to see what needs changing and more willing to do so. What's the "right" amount of time? Stephen King says six weeks. I say, however long it takes until you don't feel precious about every page. Depending on how long your book is and how much time you spent on the draft, it could be longer or shorter than that six-week benchmark.

Change the format. Sometimes we don't have the luxury of time—deadlines, contest entries, etc. get in the way. To force that objectivity, changing the format in which you're working can be helpful. I draft on my laptop, but I always revise by printing out my manuscript, three-hole-punching it, and putting it in a binder to edit by hand. Holding the physical printed page and seeing the words offscreen gives me the distance I need to tackle big edits. A member of my critique group will sometimes print her manuscript out in landscape mode, in two columns, as though it were a paperback book. These visual tricks fool our brains into separating our drafting effort from our editing energy. It can be exactly what we need.

Read it, record it. Although this is a variation on changing format, I believe it deserves its own section. Reading our work aloud uses different parts of our brain, and hearing our work allows us to catch errors more quickly than seeing them on the page. Most native English speakers are able to easily identify grammatical mistakes when they hear them, so if grammar is an area that's a challenge for you, this is a way to overcome it. Reading aloud forces us to pay attention to each word, the length of our sentences, and the tone of our pieces. Listening quickly shows us where we get bored, what elements fall flat, and where words repeat. I'll frequently read parts of my manuscripts out loud, whispering to myself in a cafe, library, or my living room, to see how sections sound. Inevitably, I catch different errors when I do this than when I'm just reading to myself off the page.

—————

CULTIVATING objectivity isn't quite enough, however. It helps us get a couple of tentacles in the box, but there are still more to wrestle into place.

The next step is to come up with a game plan or approach to your revision. Before I start making any changes, I figure out *how* I am going to revise. If you're someone who finds revision overwhelming, or you aren't sure where to start, adding a planning step before revising can be very helpful.

The good news is, there are several directions in which to go. Some writers decide that they are going to go through the book chapter by chapter, beginning to end, reading and making notes and changes. Some decide to set up a list of things that they *know* they have to fix, before they even read a word. Other writers choose an element—tracking a character, following a specific plot thread or theme—and follow it through the manuscript, changing that piece only. There is no "right" way to do this, and it will likely change from book to book. However, you have to figure out which route you're going to take. What one makes sense to you, intuitively? Whichever it is, go with that.

Once you decide on your approach, my other suggestion is to read through the manuscript once, from beginning to end, *without making a mark or a change.* This is so you can have a sense of the whole book before you dive in. You'll refresh yourself on the cat you added in chapter five, or the cousin who made an appearance in chapter twenty. You'll find some passages that are as clunky as your older brother's high school hunk-of-junk car, and some that make you feel *so* sad, or laugh *so* hard, you'll wonder if you really wrote them. Enjoy the experience of reading the thing you wrote...and then dive in and get that octopus tucked into the box.

CHAPTER 18

LET'S GET QUIRKY

ONCE I RECEIVE FEEDBACK AND START PUTTING THE octopus in the box, I inevitably get to a point in the revision process where I'm totally stymied. I've Done All the Things, Made All the Changes, but the book *still isn't right*, and I'm missing something.

This is when I need to get quirky.

At a conference I attended, author Kate Messner gave a talk about revision. She mentioned that there are certain elements in the revision process that each book needs, that perhaps wouldn't be applicable to other novels we've written. I've seen this borne out again and again. I call it the Quirky Revision Technique.

Once I get to the point where I need to figure out what that quirky thing is, I get super excited—because I also know that employing this element is going to make the manuscript take a big leap in terms of its quality, and it's going to solve some of the remaining pesky problems I'm dealing with.

So what's the difference between quirky revision and regular revision?

Let's get weird.

In "regular" revision, you may be making notes, deleting scenes or sections. Maybe you've printed your manuscript, maybe you're doing it all on screen—either way, that's fine.

Quirky happens when we lift the manuscript out of its actual form and employ completely new ways of seeing our story.

Visual methods. Seeing your book as a whole can be really helpful: You can shrink your manuscript font size, and color code it by point of view character, or highlight plot threads in different colors. This shows you very quickly where your imbalances lie and holes appear. You can hang the whole manuscript up on a wall and move pieces around, to better see how they fit. You can even use color-coded index cards (virtual or real), summarize events on them, and lay them out to see how threads move through your story. All of these will give you a very obvious way to "see" what's missing in your manuscript.

Timelines and calendars. Maybe your book takes place over a big stretch of time or is compressed into a span of days or weeks. Either way, perhaps a calendar or timeline is what you need: Plot out your events and when big story moments happen. Character going to school on a Saturday? Whoops! Miss a major holiday that would give them time off? Gotta fix that. You can also see if what you've set up is possible within the story's timeframe.

Charts. Maybe you need to plan some stuff out: seating charts for the book that takes place in a classroom, tide charts for that mystery that happens at the seaside resort, weather charts, a list of how much allowance your character has spent/earned over the course of the story. Sometimes, a well-designed chart reveals all kinds of logistical information that we weren't aware of.

Maps. Where does your story take place? If you're writing a quest-based fantasy, you may want to map out your characters' routes. Topographical maps, road maps, neighborhood maps, maps of spaces—homes, schools, office buildings—all provide precise visual elements for grounding us and our readers in our stories.

Grids. I've taken giant sheets of paper, made a slew of columns and rows, and listed chapter numbers across the top and important elements down the side. These elements can be character traits, minor characters, themes...anything that I want to "track" through the book. Then I go through the story and make a check mark in the column for each chapter in which that element appears. I'm left with a big grid, where I can quickly see that I stopped mentioning the little brother in chapter 6, and he doesn't come back until chapter 15. Maybe you are writing a mystery and you need to track suspects and clues—this method could be worth a try.

Storyboards. You don't have to be an illustrator to use this method. Draw one box per chapter, or one box per scene. Illustrate (stick figures are fine) the "big moment" that's happening. You can "see" your book play out visually. If it's not interesting to look at, you need to amp up the tension or action.

There are as many different revision elements as there are books and writers. The key is to take a look at the book you have created, and figure out what the thing is that will allow you to access the pieces of the book that are harder to get to by traditional text-based editing techniques.

Be quirky. Get weird.

COMMUNITY

CHAPTER 19

PIZZA NIGHT

Thursday nights at my house are Pizza Night. That's the night I duck out to meet with my critique group, and my family has homemade pizza for dinner.

At seven pm every other Thursday night for about twenty years (!), I've had a standing date with my group, which is snazzily called Writing Group. This collection of like-minded souls has been there for me since I was single, through my wedding, the birth of my two children, getting an agent, the publishing of all of my novels and picture books, and now we are helping one another learn how to self-publish, which is why you're reading this book.

In the previous century, I worked for Houghton Mifflin Publishing Company, and a colleague swung by my desk one day and said that he'd heard I was a writer, and would I like to join a group that met on Thursday evenings? I was wrapping up grad school and knew I needed another community for accountability, so I agreed.

We met in the conference room at Houghton—although not everyone in the group worked there—until we all left the company. Then we tried other places, nomad-like, until we ended up settling on our current plan: meeting for dinner in Brookline, Massachusetts (convenient for all of us traveling from our various jobs), and critiquing our work over a meal. Many times, we head to the local ice cream place to wrap up.

Members have come and gone, but there's a core group of us who have stayed for decades. We are friendly with one another, but not all best friends. The glue that binds us is our desire to support one another's writing endeavors in the best way we can.

This community has been a critical part of my growth as a creative person. They believe in my ability. They encourage me to write. They have lifted me up when I've received rejections, my editor left, books went out of print, or yet another editor left. They push me to write better, to dig deeper into my stories. They offer helpful feedback and don't tear my work down. I trust them to tell me how to make my manuscripts stronger and to point out what's not working.

Our situation is unusual. Most critique groups don't last half as long as we have. I think our longevity has to do with several different, but important, factors:

We have different personalities and goals, but a common purpose. This group is focused on supporting our writing lives. Not everyone is pursuing traditional publication, and we don't all write in the same genre or for the same audience, but we are all willing to do our best to help the other members feel successful in the execution of their stories.

We take stock. One of our members has a second job where she does a lot of communication facilitation. She's shared some of her skills with us, and we periodically meet without a critiquing agenda, but a let's-take-stock-and-see-how-we're-doing plan. We launch projects (such as learning about indie publishing) and set aside an annual meeting to discuss our individual writing goals and assess what did or didn't work for us in the previous year.

We give space. Various members have gotten married, had kids, taken on graduate school, etc...and they take a leave of absence and come back (or sometimes they don't). That's okay. If you need to skip a couple of weeks, that's okay. No one is going to make you feel bad or judge you.

We hold members accountable. If it's your turn to submit, and you don't have anything, you're still responsible for the meeting time. Maybe you share an article or a writing exercise instead. This way, we don't lose momentum as a group.

Writing is a solitary endeavor. You sit at a keyboard and make the story work. Having a community of people around you is important. It's preparation for working with editors and agents (see "How to Receive Critique"). But mostly, it's just...nice to have people to hang out with who "get it," who understand what it's like to wrestle a story on paper and be as involved with imaginary people's problems as you are with your own.

Finding that community can be difficult, and I'd urge you to keep trying. Personalities have to click; a purpose has to be defined; trust has to be earned; lots of things come into play in order for a group to be successful. But it's definitely possible and totally worth it—and your family will love having pizza without you.

CHAPTER 20

A PARTICULAR SET OF SKILLS

You know that Liam Neeson movie, *Taken*? The one where he tells the bad guys that he has "a particular set of skills?"

That line makes me think of my critique group.

We are not a group of crack ex-military professionals who will do damage if you come our way, but we do have specific skill sets.

We have a member who is great at identifying stereotypes, racial issues, and problematic social tropes. We have another one who excels in assessing story logic. Another is a wordsmither, who identifies repeated words, flabby verbs, and repeated sentence structure, and so on. We're all good at assessing character, discussing motivation, pacing, and plot. We can all converse about themes and arcs, too. I feel confident that when I hand over whatever it is I'm working on, I am going to get an effective, thoughtful critique.

Each of us has a particular lens through which we view other people's writing. Figuring out your strength is important, but learning to shore up areas where you're not as strong is also useful.

How do you develop these skills? The short answer: by critiquing other people's work and reading a lot. We've already discussed the critique part, but the reading part is equally important.

In teaching circles, we refer to books that we use when we're showing students how a specific author executes a craft element as mentor texts. Mentor texts are incredibly powerful tools. Many of us have several different possible mentor texts in our homes and can get even more with a quick trip to the library.

There are a couple of ways to use mentor texts. The first is straightforward: Choose a book that you like that is similar to yours in genre, or theme, or audience—something that crosses with your story—and read it (or re-read it, as the case may be). Then, look for the element you want to learn from. Is the plot particularly fast-paced? Does the writer make it impossible for you to put it down? How is that done? Look at the chapter endings and beginnings.

Is there something about the character that's extra compelling? Identify where you first felt that way. Why? What type of description is the writer using?

If you're using a book that belongs to you, dust off your skills from school. Take notes; write in the margins. Grab a highlighter and mark passages that resonate. Litter it with sticky notes. In order to learn from the story, you have to engage with it.

I was trying to work on pacing for a novel, so I took my mentor text and a big sheet of paper and literally made a chart of when the action rose and fell, how long each chapter was, and how much information was conveyed. This exercise, of deconstructing someone else's book, gave me a deeper understanding as to how to build my own.

Another way to use a mentor text is to take a book that *didn't* work for you, and pull that apart. Were the characters flat? Maybe the plot had a hole in it that you couldn't get past, or the logic seemed off. Take a deeper dive into it and try to figure out where the mistakes were, or what made the book ineffective for you. Then assess how you'd fix it. This is teaching you story logic—and also the complexities of manipulating many story lines, because inevitably, whatever you touch on one thread reverberates through the whole book.

While all of this is going on—the deconstructing, the writing in the margins, the sticky notes waving like neon flags—your brain is absorbing how the story works. The next time you critique your own piece, or someone else's, you'll be looking with sharper eyes. And the more you do this, the more your own particular set of skills will develop.

CHAPTER 21

BE A JOINER

THERE'S A ROMANTIC VISION OF A WRITER IN A GARRET, pecking out words on their typewriter and sending them off into the world with a hope and a prayer. The truth is, publishing is a business, your words are your product, and navigating the road of taking care of your intellectual property can be a big undertaking.

This is where professional organizations and collectives come in really handy.

There are organizations for just about every genre category and readership, and these professional groups offer a lot of support and benefits in return for their membership fees.

When I really committed to getting published and getting my career off the ground, the first group I sought out was the Society of Children's Book Writers and Illustrators (SCBWI). This international organization has chapters in nearly every state, regional conferences, and two big annual conferences (winter in NYC and summer in Los Angeles). SCBWI supports pre-published writers as they find their way through the process of finding publishing success and published authors in their careers. I attended the New England regional conference for a few years and have been a presenter for the past ten years. The NESCBWI conference is where I found my people—other children's book writers. These authors and illustrators understood what I was trying to do and related to what I was talking about—I felt seen in a way I never had before. I made dear friends through those conferences, and I'm so grateful to be involved in evolving roles with the organization. Published luminaries, newbies, hot commodity up-and-comers—everyone mingles and learns from one another. The weekend conference is packed with sessions on everything from formatting a query letter to developing characters and how to run an effective school visit. There are regional and national awards voted on by paying members, and these peer-selected honors are meaningful and significant.

Other organizations exist for mystery writers (Mystery Writers of America), sci-fi (Science Fiction Writers of America), romance (Romance Writers of America), and so on. Indie authors have their own organizations, too. The benefit of belonging to these organizations is that you have a place to go for information. Publishing seems like a mysterious process, but these groups will pull back the curtain and show you the steps you need to take on this journey. I cannot stress how important they are.

I value community so much that I've also been honored to join the board of a local writing non-profit, The Writers' Loft in Sherborn, MA. The Loft offers classes, workshops, critique groups, and all sorts of opportunities for members to connect and ask questions. There's a physical space in which one can write (pre-Covid, I used to go quite often), and now that we're in the midst of the pandemic, all of their workshops and classes have moved online. There are other places—another Loft (no connection) in Minnesota, the Writing Barn in Austin, Texas, Grub Street in Boston, Massachusetts, the Highlights Foundation in Pennsylvania, and Gotham City Writers in NYC. A quick Internet search will likely turn up dozens more; there's bound to be something near you. These spaces are ones where you can learn, connect, and grow as a writer. You can educate yourself about our industry.

Conferences and retreats are another way to cultivate community. I try to attend one or two conferences or retreats per year. Some are geared toward developing my craft, others are just about large blocks of writing time—both of which I need regularly.

The dues for these organizations and the cost of retreat or conference attendance can add up. Choose wisely, but recognize that these are investments in your career that will pay dividends long after you come home.

The longer I'm in this field, the more I realize that so much of it is about growth and education. The authors who study craft, learn from one another, and are open to being better writers, are the ones whose careers have longevity. Not everyone can be a bestseller, so it's up to us to learn about all of the ways we can do our work and take it to our readers. Don't miss that opportunity.

You may wish you could have the writer's life up in the garret, but the reality of 21st century authorship is far from that isolated space. Connecting with a community of like-minded people who do the thing that you do and can teach you to do it even better is going to make it easier and more joyful.

PUBLISHING

CHAPTER 22

DON'T QUIT YOUR DAY JOB

IN GRADUATE SCHOOL, MY PROFESSOR BROUGHT AN AUTHOR to speak to our class. She was an Edgar Award winner, had a successful career, and...a day job?

"Don't rely on your creative work to pay the bills," she said. "Don't force it to do that."

Now, I know several writers who have been able to leave their day jobs and write full-time—but that is not the norm. Most of us have day jobs. My husband is a freelancer, and I have a full-time job as a professor. My college teaching gig provides health insurance for our family.

I won't lie—working full time, raising two kids, and writing a book a year is not easy—but I wouldn't have it any other way. Here's why:

Publishing advances are paid out over time, in chunks. Some publishers pay in halves, others in thirds (and post-Covid, my guess is we'll see more payments in thirds or maybe even quarters). The first third is upon signing the contract, the second is when the manuscript is "delivered and accepted," and the last is when the book is released.

Contracts can take upwards of six months to negotiate.

"Delivered and accepted" could mean your first turn in of the manuscript, or the last round of edits before copyedits. Your contract will specify this. There could be as many as six months in this window.

Release date? A year or two after the manuscript is accepted.

Deduct fifteen percent for your agent (who earns every penny), a chunk depending on what tax bracket you fall into (yes—you now have to pay quarterly taxes, so set that cash aside!), and you can see how quickly a $100,000 advance turns into three payments of about $22,000—over eighteen months. That's nothing to sneeze at, for sure. But most writers aren't making six-figure advances, either.

In order to sustain a career this way, you need to produce work at a fast rate, sell it for sizable advances, and have your books earn out (earn back their advances), so that royalty checks come in to supplement the gaps between advance payments, and then add a layer of speaking engagements or school visits (if you write for kids) for steady income. And, as we've seen, throw in a global pandemic, and many of the speaking engagements and school visits disappear. It took a few months for organizations to figure out how to make their programs go virtual, and that meant three to five months of lost income for many creative people.

Not all, but many of the full-time writers that I know have spouses whose jobs give them health insurance and a steady, consistent paycheck. If you have a family, or have chronic issues that require higher levels of care, take a serious look at whether being a full-time writer makes sense for you and your lifestyle.

The other advantage to holding a day job: You aren't relying on your creative life to provide the elements you need to sustain the lifestyle you want. When your passion becomes necessary to your survival, all of a sudden you start making decisions and choices that maybe you don't want to have to make, like setting aside that project you love to do a six-week turnaround write-for-hire book. If the crush to get that write-for-hire book finished burns you out and sets you further behind on the book you *want* to write, or you write faster to generate more income, but your craft suffers and your work isn't strong, that's a really difficult trade-off to have to make.

This also means that you get to have a job that isn't your main source of fulfillment and joy. Maybe it's something 9-5 that you can walk away from at the end of the day and not think about until you clock in the next morning. Perhaps it's a part-time gig at a company that gives you health insurance, or hours that match your kids' school day, so you can be home when they are. There's nothing wrong with working while writing, no matter how many books you've published.

Personally, I'm not sure that I would enjoy the life of a full-time writer. Teaching gives me energy, and being in the classroom, talking about books and writing, makes me happy. It also forces me to constantly examine my craft and stay on top of industry news. Does it take time outside of the 9-5 day? You bet it does. But I don't have class every day; I do have vacations and summers off; and I am fortunate to work at a college with a mission to bring creativity into the world. My writing is supported and encouraged there.

For some reason, we think we need oodles of time at our disposal to achieve a goal or follow our passions. I know if I had all day to write, I wouldn't write all day. I'd write for a little bit, and then I'd do laundry, futz around on the Internet, take a walk, or organize my sock drawer. Scarcity of time is one of my motivators. I have to use those hours well when I have them, and I get far more done that way. I like to think that I dream big but live realistically.

CHAPTER 23

THE BEST FRIENDS NECKLACE: FINDING AN AGENT

I'LL BE PRESENTING AT A CONFERENCE, TALKING ABOUT revision or dialogue or one of the other craft elements in this book, and it comes over a few faces: The flicker of impatience, a shadow of annoyance. *Here we go*, I think. I finish my talk, click my "thank you" slide up on the screen, and say, "Let's open it up to questions."

The hands go up.

"But how do you get an agent?" they say, the annoyance and impatience replaced by eager eyes and poised pencils. "Tell us."

What I usually say is along the lines of "write well, query, patience, query...rinse and repeat" in an upbeat, encouraging manner.

What I want to say is this:

There is definitely a path to traditional publishing, and it is open to you if you have patience and work on your craft. But there are no shortcuts or magic steps to bring you to the front of the line. If you want to pursue traditional publishing, you need an agent. Here's what it takes to get one:

1. Write well. This is the thing above all else. Your writing needs to be as good as you can possibly make it. Solid story arcs, characters who grow and change, a compelling voice, a grounded setting...All the Things. And honestly, lots of times our writing isn't where it needs to be by the time we start querying. You may be feeling antsy because you've been working on this project for *so long*, or you've gotten hooked into the industry enough to see what is selling—and you inevitably think, *my book sounds just as cool/cooler than that!*—or you simply want to move on to the next thing and get this one out the door. Don't. Just...don't. Your book needs more time, I guarantee you. Let it sit. Show it to your critique group again. Better yet, show it to another writer who is not in your critique group. Let it sit some more. Work on something else. Work on it some more. It's not ready.

2. Research. While you're letting it sit or working on your next project, you need to do some research. Subscribe to the free Publisher's Weekly newsletters, so you can read about what's happening in your industry and learn about what books are selling and which agents are representing them. Now is also the time to join that genre organization, if you haven't yet. Go to the library. Read books that are similar to yours, and jot down which agents represented them (authors always thank their agents in the acknowledgements). Go to agents' websites. Start making lists of people whom you might want to work with. Listen to podcasts and follow these people on social media. The more research you put in, the better your chances of developing a list of people who will be interested in what you're writing. The added benefit is that you are learning more about the industry.

3. Make the list. Set up some sort of tracking system—a spreadsheet, a Word doc, or even a spread in your notebook. You'll want to list the agent's name, the agency they work for, contact info/submission info, what you sent, and when you sent it. The last couple of columns should be when you hear back and any notes they send. An important note: Every agent has different requirements for what you should submit and how. It's usually found on their website or social media. Follow their rules. If one asks for two chapters and you send five, because everyone else wants five, you are giving that agent an easy reason to say "no thanks" to you.

4. Write the query letter. To introduce yourself to an agent, you write what's called a query letter. There are tons of resources for how to best do this, so I'll just keep it brief. You want to keep it to one page and three paragraphs: The first paragraph is about your book; the second paragraph is about why you want to work with the agent; and the third paragraph is about you. You are not as important as your story, which is why we're putting your biographical info last ("I'm a writer and teacher from Kalamazoo, and *Biker Gang Space Invaders* is my first book"). Take *a lot* of time to get your letter right: Check your spelling and grammar. Keep it short. Be detailed. And lastly—it's ok to give away the ending. There's no reason for secrecy. Your agent wants to know that you can finish a book and bring it to a good conclusion.

5. Check your book again. Yes, I know. But why blow your first impression? Take the time to look at those first 50 pages like you've never seen them before. Are they as tight and good as they can be? Does your book start in the right place? Have you pulled in your reader? If so…start submitting to the names on your list. I worked in batches, sending out 3-5 queries at a time. You may do more or less, depending on how long your list is.

6. Wait and record. Get a response with a personal note? Make sure you record that info. A flat-out rejection? That's okay. Dust off and keep going. Rejection is part of the business, and it means that our work is out there, getting responses.

7. Keep your chin up. Once you start querying, it feels like you're standing in (pre-Covid-19) Times Square, with one half of a best friends necklace, stopping random people to see if the half they have matches yours. It can be lonely and discouraging. It can take time, and it requires perseverance and patience. You have both of these things. Keep trying.

8. Assess. If you've sent out a bunch of queries and haven't received any requests for partials or personal responses, it may be time to assess your manuscript. What's "a bunch", you ask? It depends. For me, if I sent out ten and didn't hear anything, I'd reassess. This is because if you've done your research well, honed in on your writing and perfected your query letter, you should get a personal response or some requests.

Remember: There's no magic, shortcuts, or sidesteps, just patience and hard work. Hang in there, and I hope you find your perfect match!

CHAPTER 24

WAITING IS THE HARDEST PART: HOW SUBMISSIONS WORK

Wahooo!! You've signed with an agent! This is super exciting. Now, after getting to know one another and working together a little bit (and revising that manuscript *one more time*), your book is winging its way to editors. You're On Submission.

Now what?

You wait. Being on submission can mean waiting for a long time (months), or it can happen fast (a matter of days, if your book is a super hot commodity, or the stars align just right). Publishing gives us lots of opportunities to practice patience.

When my work is newly out on submission, I refresh my email like it's my part-time job. I'll check out the editors' social media feeds, seeing if I can glean whether or not they've read my manuscript, based on their food posts or pictures of their cat. I may or may not light candles and float around like Stevie Nicks in a 1980s video, sending positive vibes into the universe.

I'm not proud of this behavior.

But I also recognize that it's natural. After all, this is a Big Moment. My book has to stand on its own, with support from my agent, and someone else has to fall in love with it.

After three hardcore days of living in a state of suspended anxiety, I come back to myself, put my floaty scarves away, and remember that no matter how many vibes I send out, I cannot influence anything at this point.

So, I do what I always do: Get back to work. The work is the part of this journey over which I have the most influence. Typically, before I'm on sub, I'm working on another project, so that's what I get back into. It's hard to concentrate on it at first, because my brain and heart are with that other manuscript, wondering what the editors are thinking, if someone is reading it *right now*, if it's making them laugh? Should I have taken out that scene with the cow? And on and on.

Focus. Breathe.

The current project needs me. I am a better writer working on this new project than I was on the project that's on sub right now, and this could be the next book that an editor buys. They'll want a two-book deal, right? So I need to finish this one....Wait. Are they reading the other one now?

You see how it goes. It's the epitome of the Monkey Mind. Ultimately, though, I *do* get myself together and settle down. I know what is going on behind the scenes, and selling a book takes time.

The editor has to read it. Now, depending on what kind of book you're submitting, it might have a *lot* of pages. And the editor has to read it *all*. Even if it's short, the editor still needs time to think about it. And your book isn't the only one they've received this week, or month, so there's definitely a stack they have to get through. Plus, they have to do the rest of their job. Editors don't sit around reading all day (that would be my dream job!). They're working on the books they're publishing, sending some to copyedits, checking page proofs for ones that are already designed, meeting with art directors to talk about covers or finding an illustrator for a specific project, meeting with their team to discuss what's coming out next, talking with marketing about a big book that releases next year...etc. etc. They are *busy*. They sometimes read those submissions on their own time—nights, weekends, while commuting (on the train, of course!). Maybe they take a coffee break and read the first ten pages of three books, to prioritize which order to finish the rest, or knock them from consideration entirely. Unless your book is in an auction (more on that in a second), there is not an absolute rush to get to it.

Once the editor reads and falls in love with your story, there are still more steps. Now, things can go in a couple of directions at this point. One direction is that the editor loves it, but they want the writer (you) to make a few tweaks, so they will ask your agent how you feel about that, and your agent will ask you. If you agree, then the editor might send the agent or you an email with their requests, or maybe you'll talk on the phone and go over a few things. Then you make the changes.

The other direction is that the editor feels the book is in good enough shape as-is, and they will take it to their acquisitions meeting. You may or may not know this is happening to your manuscript. A little-known piece of info about how publishing works: Few editors get to make unilateral decisions about what books they buy. The publisher or imprint will have a regularly scheduled meeting (weekly, monthly, or on an ad-hoc basis), when the staff get together and discuss the books that they are excited about buying. Now, if two editors in the same house or imprint show up with similar manuscripts—biker gang vampire novels, for example—it isn't likely that both will be acquired, so those editors duke it out. This is one reason why your book has to be in the best shape possible—you want it to win if there is an Editorial Throwdown. There are also other factors that go in to editors choosing certain books over others: they may have a specific budget they're working with, or their house or imprint has its own tone—a book, no matter how good, no matter how much the editor wants it, has to fit.

If you know your book is on an acquisitions agenda, it is totally appropriate to bust out your Stevie Nicks moves, candles, and eat a lot of chocolate on Acquisitions Meeting Day.

If your book is a Super Hot Commodity of Awesomeness, and you had multiple agents fall over themselves bringing you flowers and candy for the privilege of representing your work, your manuscript may end up in an auction. This is whole different experience.

The agent sends the manuscript out. Then, multiple editors respond quickly. There's a lot of excitement for the book. At that point, the agent sets up a deadline by which all interested parties have to read the manuscript and submit their bids. Auctions happen, but they don't happen for every manuscript. If your book goes to auction, you are likely to have a different publishing experience than the majority of writers, which is awesome for you. Acquisitions through auctions typically come with higher advances, a larger marketing budget, and more expectations on the author. This is when your relationship with your agent becomes critical, as you will need them by your side to navigate those waters.

Whether your book experiences a standard acquisitions process or an auction, it will be rejected by some of the people who read it (to soften the blow, editors refer to this as "declining"). This is okay. This is where separating ourselves from our work is critical. No one is rejecting you as a person—this *book* just isn't for them or their house/imprint. It can sting, but the best thing you can do is acknowledge it and get back to work. Your book will find the people who love it, and you will make something new and wonderful.

And hey—keep those floaty scarves and candles handy for the next time you're on submission.

CHAPTER 25

SIMMER DOWN, GUNPOWDER: MANAGING EXPECTATIONS

You've signed with an agent! Maybe they've sold your book! Hooray!! This is super, super exciting. You need to celebrate. Have something fizzy or chocolate, treat yourself to that massage or tattoo or whatever it is you've attached to this day. You have achieved a dream, and that's an amazing accomplishment. I am thrilled for you.

Now, let's get real.

Go re-read the "Don't Quit Your Day Job" section. I'll wait.

Okay.

A lot of stuff is going to come at you pretty soon: Author questionnaires from the marketing department. An editorial letter (more than one). Marketing plans. People whom you don't know—*whom you likely have never even met in person!*—are going to be reading your book and telling you how excited they are to publish it.

They *are* very excited.

They can't wait to work with you.

But—and I need to be completely honest here, because you've read this far, and we're friends now—I need to tell you to manage your expectations.

This dream-being-achieved thing is heady stuff. Our fingertips tingle; our heart races. There's so much *possibility*. Depending on your agent and book, there could be a lot of big numbers being thrown around, promises about marketing plans and promotion, and bonuses built into your contract. And this is wonderful, amazing, and exciting—and you should savor every second of it.

But also know this: Your book is not the only one they are publishing. Your book, wonderful and special as it may be, is perhaps not the only wonderful and special one on the publisher's list for that season. There is a lot of work left to do, and a lot will be expected of you.

You need to market your book and connect with readers and reviewers. You need to network with your potential audience— perhaps that's teachers and librarians, if you write for kids. Or, if you're writing for adults, it's book clubs and fans of specific genres. This is where all of the work you've done in networking in the organizations you've joined starts to pay off.

You joined an organization, right?

You have a community and other writers who you can reach out to, right?

As your book moves through the editorial process and gets closer to publication, there are decisions you will make, decisions other people will make for your book, and decisions that will surprise you. This is all normal. I've had publishers show me elaborate marketing plans for a book, only to have them acquire something so big and exciting that a portion of the budget allotted to my book gets moved to support that Really Big Book. I have writer friends who have hated their covers, or whose back-cover copy doesn't actually describe their stories. Or, there's a global pandemic when your debut novel drops, and literally every bookstore in a 200-mile radius is closed. This happens. And it's hard and disappointing and can leave you feeling like a shell of a human.

This is why we celebrate and get the tattoo and do all of the other things to mark The Moment...because once The Moment passes, you are In Business. You are In Business with a publisher who wants to make money, and your book is the product that they sell by which to do that.

This is okay. This is how things work.

What we have to do—what we *get* to do, when we work hard and are fortunate and get to this point—is double down on the things we *can* do. We can be excited, share our enthusiasm, work on our revisions, and, most importantly, start our next project.

It's our next projects that allow us to do it all again.

LIFE STUFF

CHAPTER 26

15 MINUTES COULD SAVE YOU

That gecko on the car insurance commercial extolls how much money he can save for you in fifteen minutes or less. While I know nothing about car insurance or small reptiles, I *do* know what fifteen minutes can do for you.

Fifteen minutes can make you a writer.

Fifteen minutes can help you finish that book.

Fifteen minutes can be the difference between achieving your dream or not.

That's all: fifteen minutes.

I may not sit down and write every day, but I can just about always find fifteen minutes to grab a pen and my notebook.

Here's what I may do with that time:

1. Freewrite about my project, assessing where I am and what the story needs.

2. Freewrite about how busy I am, and how I'm struggling to find the time I need.

3. Make a list of what comes next in my book.

4. Draw my main character (poorly, awkwardly).

5. Sketch the book's setting (poorly, awkwardly).

6. Make a web of plot elements and how they connect to character.

7. Write a letter from my character to me, so they can tell me what I need to hear.

8. Work on a plot problem or a character's needs.

9. Make a continuity list, so I have the names of classes, school, places the characters frequent, eye color, hair color, etc. all in one place.

10. Plan out my writing time for the rest of the week.

11. Reread other things I've written in my notebook.

━━━

THESE FIFTEEN MINUTES keep my head in the world of the story, which helps maintain momentum. Writing when my kids were infants and pre-schoolers, I learned quickly that I couldn't wait for a muse or for large, uninterrupted stretches of time to do work. That was a luxury that my first colicky, cranky kid wasn't going to afford me. I had to work when I could—and sometimes that was only for fifteen minutes. But that's enough, if you do it regularly. If you use the fifteen minutes on the days when you can't carve out extra time, there's an internal pressure, an eagerness, that builds and builds until you *can't wait* to sit down on Saturday morning, or Thursday night, or Wednesday afternoon.

Am I always doing this, every single day, one hundred percent of the time? No. I forget. I stop. I fall out of the practice. But when I'm doing it—when I get back on that horse—I am always reminded of how easy it is and how good it feels...and *how much easier it becomes to work on my book.*

There is no other way around writing except to write. There are no shortcuts or ways to circumvent this process. We must sit and write one word at a time. However, there are ways to make those words come a little faster, a little easier, and to make those larger swaths of time that we do have available more effective. Taking even fifteen minutes to work on your craft and get into the world of your story, pays huge dividends.

Your car insurance? That's a whole other issue.

CHAPTER 27

THE JUGGLE IS REAL

I'M A MOM OF TWO, A WIFE, A COLLEGE PROFESSOR, A writer, and we have a grumpy dog. My husband is a freelancer, so my job provides our health insurance and a stable base salary for our family. My first book released when my oldest was ten months old. Although I had years of being child-free while writing, my career didn't truly start until my kids were in the picture.

And man, was I tired. I still am.

Being a parent and a writer is hard. Being a mom and a writer—some may say it's an even more difficult lift. Taking time away from the small people (sometimes *very* small people) in your life to lock yourself in a room (or escape to a library or coffee shop) and sit with your laptop and imaginary friends can feel selfish and indulgent.

But I realized pretty quickly that writing makes me a better mom, wife, and professor. When I am not writing, my temper is shorter, and my patience frays more easily. I'm not bringing what I know into the classroom. I'm not walking the walk.

I want my children to see that I value my writing. I want them to watch me carve out time to do work that is creative and for others (and myself). It's hard, but it's also necessary.

The question is, how do writer-parents find the time to create, raise their families, and work?

I will point out: Male authors are rarely asked this question.

A highly successful author-illustrator who I know once described a relationship in conjunction with his own as "creator and enabler." This person postulated that every creative person needs someone who enables them to be creative—the enabler handles the "little bits" of daily life that would bog down the creative.

Wouldn't that be nice?

In truth, it's messy around here. Literally and figuratively.

We were fortunate in that we had help from grandparents when our kids were little, and on the days I went to school, my mother or my mother-in-law came and took care of our kids. We didn't have the expense of daycare, and my children have wonderful relationships with their grandparents. I realize how privileged that is, and I'm tremendously grateful for their help.

So my school days were covered, but I don't write during my school days—I teach, run a department of 20 faculty members, and oversee our college's curriculum for liberal arts. Writing happens at other times.

I don't write every day—with my day job, I can't. On my non-teaching days, when my kids were little (three or four books' worth), I wrote at night, going out after dinner a couple of nights per week. I'd also go out on the weekends for a few hours, spending time at a local cafe down the street. When my oldest started second grade, and my youngest started preschool, I nearly wept with joy for the three hours, twice a week, I'd have with no kids at home. Sometimes, I packed up the kids and spent a weekend with my parents. They'd get grandparent time, while I'd steal a few hours in the basement, working on a manuscript.

Did I mention that all this time, my oldest didn't sleep through the night?

I don't say all of this to be like, "Look what I did, I'm so awesome," but to show that it is *not* easy. I was exhausted. I couldn't take on as many school visits or travel as much as other authors. A couple of times each year, I'd go to a conference, or later, go on a writing retreat weekend with friends, but those were rare. It was super hard. It still is.

My husband is a wonderful partner, who competently and confidently manages the kids and dog while I'm not home. He also vacuums, which is a bonus.

But I'm always making tradeoffs: crockpot meatballs for dinner, a big pile of laundry to get through, the bathroom isn't sparkling, feeling guilty if I watch a movie. There's always *something* to be done, work to do, papers to grade, manuscripts to finish. I cram a lot of writing into the weeks when I'm not in school and my kids are. And as I write this, nine months into the pandemic, our previous structure and routine have been thrown out the window.

The family items that are non-negotiable: putting the kids to bed, dinners at the table as a family, helping them with their schoolwork. Once a month, we try to go someplace new (which we've even kept up during the pandemic)—a place to hike, or something to see, or whatever. It's not fancy, but it's fun.

So how do I do it? I make tradeoffs. I let stuff go. I get help from my husband and others. I work a lot. I am very, very tired.

I wouldn't trade it for the world.

CHAPTER 28

INVEST IN YOURSELF

TEN YEARS INTO MY PUBLISHING CAREER, AND I STILL
have to force myself to say the words, "I'm a writer," or "I'm an
author." Usually, when I introduce myself, I say I'm a college
professor, and I "write children's books," like it's my hobby. I
know. I know. Look, I'm giving *myself* side-eye right now.

As of 2021, I'm leading with, "I'm an author and a college
professor," because that's what I am, damn the Impostor
Syndrome.

Although I may struggle with saying it out loud, the one thing I
do *not* struggle with is taking my writing seriously. I saw the
difference between what happens when I futzed around with
my work, writing only when it was my turn to submit to my
critique group (2000-2005), and when I got serious about my
writing (2005-present). The difference: A book deal. Nine of
them.

No one comes knocking on your door at the end of the day, asking what you've written. No one is going to prod you to get to work late at night or early in the morning. So much of this journey is about self-discipline...but it's also about taking yourself seriously and investing in your dream. And investing is not an empty word. There are things we can do that show ourselves and those around us that our work is important. We can invest in time, money, and headspace. Here's how each of these items are necessary as you go on this journey and why those investments are worth it:

Time. Putting words on the page, revising, reading a craft book, meeting with your critique group, critiquing a partner's work...all of that takes time. It can take as much or as little time as you make room for—but you are the one who has to make room for it. If you aren't intentional about your writing time, I guarantee you it will get frittered away. There's laundry to be done, Netflix to watch, kids or partners to take care of/hang out with, day job work, and other things. How much time to invest is up to you—but you need to be realistic. If you have a full-time job, a family, and other obligations, writing for two hours a day is likely not going to happen. Two hours on a weekend morning? More likely. Take a realistic look at your calendar and schedule, and then plan your writing time. Hold it sacred. Don't let other obligations creep into that scheduled space. Make the commitment to yourself and your craft. Time is the one component that is nonnegotiable. You *need* to make the time if you want to write.

Money. The amount of actual money you invest can be as small as the cost of pens and a notebook, to substantial investments in software. You can choose to only spend on the tools of writing (pen, notebook, and most likely, a computer), but once you get going, there may be other items that you want to invest in to improve your process and grow your craft. Specific software programs, such as Scrivener (on which I'm writing right now), WriterDuet (great for pairs of writers working on joint projects), Highland, or Final Draft (for screenwriters), are available for purchase. Whatever comes with your laptop works, too. Other areas in which you may spend money include membership fees for organizations like (in my case) the Society of Children's Book Writers and Illustrators, Mystery Writers of America, etc. There's a list of organizations and resources you may want to consider in the "A Few of My Favorite Things" piece. I also spend money on attending conferences and writing retreats. Conferences are packed full of craft talks and provide opportunities to network and learn about the industry. Retreats are unstructured time to just write. Some writers I know do large retreats with groups of writer friends; others go alone for a weekend or two. I try to go on retreat twice a year, once in the winter and once in the late summer/early fall. Those unstructured blocks of time give me the space I need to focus on my work, not anything else. Investing money automatically makes you take your work more seriously, because you've spent hard-earned cash on it. But even if your "investment" is $4.00 at a coffee shop while you write on Saturday morning, the dividends will eventually pay off!

Headspace. Aside from time to write, having the headspace in which to think about your characters, plan for your books, and digest your story is also helpful. This is not to say you need to spend hours in a meditative state, but you do need to be able to think about your story. Sometimes that happens while you're doing the dishes or commuting. Sometimes it's in the shower. Sometimes it's just before you go to sleep at night. Any of those times are fine. The key is making sure everyday life doesn't intrude on your headspace. I'm a big fan of writing lists to get my to-dos or worries on paper, to make room in my mind for my story ideas. When I have too much going on (ok, I *always* have too much going on), I don't have room to let my subconscious work on my story. Clearing out space, giving my brain time and tools to work when we're not at the keyboard, is important.

All of this is basically code for: Value yourself. To the outsider, writing can look indulgent. To you, it may feel selfish. But the time investment to follow a dream is invaluable. If you're a parent, you're showing your kids the work it takes to pursue something you love. If you're a spouse or friend, you're showing your partners and the people in your life that you take this work seriously. And ultimately, you're showing yourself that you deserve to take this road and see where it leads.

CHAPTER 29

RUN YOUR OWN RACE

I'T'S INEVITABLE AND UNAVOIDABLE, AND IT CAN SIMMER at a low boil or hit you like a gut punch. Unless you're a rare soul, it's going to find you at some point:

Jealousy.

The little green monster pops up along the route of your writing journey with scarily reliable accuracy.

Haven't finished a book yet, and someone on social media is crowing about typing "The End"? There's the monster.

Revising, and someone in your critique group is querying? Grrr.

Querying, and literally everyone you know is getting requests for fulls, or agents offering representation like the Red Sox throwing beads off their World Series party float? Seethe.

Once you've been published, those feelings don't go away, they just level up with the situation:

- So-and-so's book gets a higher advance? Burn!

- That book gets more marketing support? UGH.

- Every single one of your friends' books ending up on Best Book of All Time lists at the end of the year, winning major awards, getting a ride at Disneyland, and plastered on the side of a spaceship? A pint of Ben & Jerry's won't cut it.

It happens. We all feel it, and depending on what our most sensitive spots are, we feel certain moments more acutely.

But here's the thing: Writing is very much a solitary sport, much like a marathon. You're in a pack of people who are all doing the same thing you are, but everyone has their own reasons for doing it, their own training regime, and some do it professionally. You are not competing against other people. No one wins.

The only person you are racing against is yourself: What do you want your experience to be like? Can you finish?

Now, I'm not a marathoner (*cackles with laughter at the thought*), but I've plodded through a 5k or two. There are people who blow by me on the course, and sometimes I need to stop or slow down, but I'm not angry at anyone for running their race. Mostly, I'm just grateful that I'm not dying on the side of the road. The sense of accomplishment I feel at the end belongs to me, for the work I've done, regardless of where I finish in the pack.

This is the mindset we need to cultivate when it comes to our writing lives. I specifically use the word "cultivate" here, the second definition of which is "to try to acquire or develop (a quality, sentiment, or skill)". Cultivating our mindset is an ongoing effort, but we are all the better for trying. If we spend time envying someone else, we take time away from our own work. Our writing is what we have control over.

Here's a truth: Some books will be better than yours. Some, that are not as good as yours, will get more attention. Do you know what you can do about it? Nothing. So write more. Get better. Maybe your next one will be the Best Thing Ever—but that doesn't matter. All that truly matters is that you create it. You can't control the outcome of anything beyond the words you put on the page.

When I feel those cold, wart-covered, green monster fingers at the back of my neck, I take a breath and step away from social media. I remind myself to keep my eyes on my own paper. I don't know that other writer's situation; I can only know my own. And it's up to me to do good work, whenever I do the work. Sometimes I have a piece of chocolate or a glass of wine.

The other thing that helps me: knowing people in the industry for whom I can be genuinely happy when good things happen to their books. It is hard to feel jealous when you know that author has struggled to get published for ten years, or they were worried that their career was dying on the vine before this book came out. Or they are simply a wonderful person who is generous with their time and spirit. I love to celebrate my writer friends' successes.

Lastly, the other thing to remember is that there are not a finite number of books that people are allowed to read, love, or share. There's always room for another good book to find an audience —whether it's an audience of millions or a handful of readers who meaningfully connect with a story. But none of that happens if you don't write your book. Or short story. Or poetry collection.

Let's agree, going forward, that we're going to lace up our sneakers, cultivate our attitude, and run our own race. We'll get a lot farther than just standing on the curb, seething, watching everyone else go by.

CHAPTER 30

VICTORY LAPS & DANCE PARTIES

WHEN WAS THE LAST TIME YOU GAVE YOURSELF A PAT ON the back for a job well done? It's so easy to get caught up in all of the "haven't dones", "didn't get tos", and stresses of everyday life that we gloss over the things that we've actually accomplished.

This goes double for our writing. It's easy to remember the rejections, or feel discouraged that you didn't finish your novel on the deadline you set, or focus on the days you didn't write this week. The problem is, the more we focus on the items we didn't get to, the worse we feel about our writing in general. And the worse we feel about writing, the less inclined we are to get back to it tomorrow.

As I've said before, writing is a solitary endeavor that requires a lot of self-discipline. But self-discipline shouldn't be confused with asceticism. Turning our creativity into a form of punishing work is nothing but a fast way to destroy ourselves. The "romantic" notion of the Suffering Artist is a myth. We don't need to suffer for our work to be good. On the contrary, as Elizabeth Gilbert points out in her TED talk about creativity, we can approach our work with joy and excitement, and *isn't that a better way to create?*

Joy doesn't just sprinkle from the clouds, however. We have to cultivate joy in our work as much as we hang on to those negative moments. This is the way we're slowly able to swap what's holding us back for what can propel us forward.

So how to do that, exactly?

First, we have to track what we accomplish. Every day that I write, I draw a star in my bullet journal. I love seeing the stars march across the top of the page. On the days I don't write, or the weeks where I'm buried in my day job and that stripe is vacant, the emptiness gently nudges me.

I added a page in my bullet journal (you can do this in a notes app or calendar) to record things I've accomplished in writing, work, and with my family. Finish a tricky chapter? I put it on the list. Finish a draft? Write it down. Seeing those items—and they can be as granular or big as I need them to be—add up provides a tremendous sense of pride and motivation. So write those successes down!

Next, make writing itself a pleasurable experience. Make your favorite tea or coffee or pour a seltzer or whatever. Light a candle, if that's your thing. Get a snack you enjoy. Find a good space to work. Good space doesn't have to be majestic or fancy —just room for what you need. Once my kids came along, I no longer had an office. I worked at the dining room table or in libraries and cafes. But what I did do was put together a "go" bag that had everything I needed in it: cables, chargers, fingerless gloves (in case wherever I was the AC was cranked in the summer, or not enough heat in winter), notebooks, printed drafts, pens. There may have been a few dark chocolate Hershey's kisses in there, too. While I'm writing this, we're still in the middle of the pandemic, and writing anywhere outside of my house is not an option. So I've designated spaces in the house where I can work: the living room, with a cozy blanket over my lap and soft music, the shared upstairs office with a closed door, my deck or porch in the nice weather. I am not precious about my space, but I am particular about it. If we enjoy the experience, we're going to want to make that time to be in that space and do the work more often.

Another important element: Celebrate the victories. Finish a chapter? Hooray! Finish a draft? Yeehaw! Give yourself rewards: a treat you like, playing a game on a device, buying a new book (preferably from an independent bookstore), a spa night (at home or at the spa, if that's your thing), a long walk, or time to yourself...whatever you do to mark special occasions. I like bakery chocolate chip cookies, balloons, and doing literal dance parties and taking victory laps around my house. *These celebrations are worthy and important.* Cheering ourselves on is how we sustain this endeavor and finish our projects. Plus, *hello!* It's a big deal to finish a chapter, a draft, or a revision! These are big moments and are worthy of acknowledgement.

This is also important once you start querying or become published. There's enough opportunity for discouragement, and plenty that is out of our control, so baking in celebrations from the beginning will keep your spirits buoyed when you're struggling.

All of this also helps with the work of writing being the reward. Finishing a book doesn't make us better people. Publication doesn't solve our problems. Our worth and feelings of success have to come from within us; otherwise, we're just running on a treadmill of dissatisfaction. Finding satisfaction and joy in the creation of the work is easier said than done (see "Run Your Own Race"), but it truly is critical. Putting value to the time we take to write, rewarding ourselves when we accomplish a step on the path, and celebrating the milestones will go a long way to bringing us a whole new perspective on our work.

Now, excuse me—I'm going to have a dance party to acknowledge finishing this essay.

CHAPTER 31

NOW WHAT?

HEY, ERIN, I'VE READ THIS WHOLE BOOK. NOW WHAT?

Well, first, thanks for sticking with me. I hope this has been helpful. I hope you're able to use what we talked about to develop your craft, navigate a revision, or build a community around your writing life.

All of the conversations in this collection come back to one thing: writing. If you want to be a writer, you have to write. You have to get the words on the page. That part's not always fun, not sexy, not glamorous. There's no shortcut you can take, no magic that can do it for you.

However, there's magic *in the doing*. There's magic in a portal opening through the words on your screen, where you watch characters you've created come alive. There's magic in hearing characters' voices in a quiet moment. And the ultimate magic happens when a reader connects with the world you built in your story, one word at a time.

You can do this.

After all, you're An Athor.

A FEW OF MY FAVORITE THINGS

Craft books, books on creativity, podcasts...I listen, learn, and grow as a writer by learning from others. Here are some of my teachers and the tools I use most regularly:

CRAFT BOOKS

Cameron, Julia. *The Artist's Way: 25th Anniversary Edition*. TarcherPerigee, 2016

Crohn, Lisa. *Story Genius*. Ten Speed Press, 2016.

Gilbert, Elizabeth. *Big Magic*. Riverhead Books, 2016.

Godin, Seth. *The Practice*. Penguin Random House, 2020.

Jacobs, Denise. *Banish Your Inner Critic*. Mango, 2017.

Kelly, Heather. *Jumpstart Your Writing in 30 Days*. Pocket Moon Press, 2020.

King, Stephen. *On Writing*. Scribner, 2010.

Klein, Cheryl. *The Magic Words*. W.W. Norton & Company, 2016.

Newport, Cal. *Deep Work*. Grand Central Publishing, 2016.

Lamott, Anne. *Bird by Bird*. Anchor, 1995.

LeGuin, Ursula. Steering the Craft. Mariner Books, 2015.

Salesses, Matthew. *Craft in the Real World*. Catapult, 2021.

Tharp, Twyla. *The Creative Habit*. Simon & Schuster, 2006.

Truby, John. *The Anatomy of Story*. Faber & Faber, 2008.

VanderMeer, Jeff. *Wonderbook: The Illustrated Guide to Creating Imaginative Fiction*. Abrams, 2018.

PODCASTS

The Accidental Creative, Todd Henry

Kids Ask Authors, Grace Lin

Kidlit Women, Grace Lin

LiteratiCast, Jennifer Laughran

Magic Lessons, Elizabeth Gilbert (no longer doing new episodes, old ones are great)

Narrative Breakdown, Cheryl Klein (no longer doing new episodes, old ones are great)

Scriptnotes, John August & Craig Mazin

The Children's Book Podcast, Matthew Winner

The Moment, Brian Koppleman

The Writers' Panel, Ben Blacker

VIDEOS

On YouTube:

Michael Arndt; Beginnings: Setting the story in Motion

Tracey Baptiste, Creativity Under Pressure series

Meet the Author: Jason Reynolds (via Fairfax County Public Schools)

TED Talks (go to Ted.com and search for these):

Chimamanda Adichie, The Danger of a Single Story

Amy Tan, Where does Creativity Hide?

JJ Abrams, The Mystery Box

Elizabeth Gilbert, Your Elusive Creative Genius

DIGITAL HELPERS

Apps that may help you organize your workflow or take care of some logistics:

Evernote—organizing notes from conferences

Final Draft –for screenplays

Highland –for screenplays

Scrivener –digital drafting

Trello—kind of like sticky notes and a big whiteboard, but on your computer

Writer Duet – for working with a partner

MATERIALS

Traditional materials to help you explore your creativity during the writing process:

Big paper

Notebooks

Graph paper

Bright colored pens/crayons/markers

Binder

Three hole punched manuscript

Highlighters

Post-Its

Imagination

Flexibility

ORGANIZATIONS

Alliance of Independent Authors

Authors' Guild

Gotham Writers' Workshop

Grub Street Writers, Boston, MA

Mystery Writers of America

Society of Children's Book Writers & Illustrators (SCBWI)

The Writers' Loft, Sherborn Massachusetts

The Writing Barn, Austin, TX

ACKNOWLEDGMENTS

If you've read this collection, you know that making it was *not* a solo endeavor. I am forever grateful to my husband, Frank, for cheering me on and encouraging me to write, even when it's hard. I am also thankful for our kids, for never complaining when Mom heads off to do "another book thing." I love you all.

Nancy Werlin, Loree Griffin Burns, and Chris Tebbetts took time to give feedback on some of the pieces in this collection. They are fantastic writers and even better friends. Go check out their websites and buy their books.

Karen Boss not only wrote the foreward but also critiqued one of the essays. She is a gifted editor and champion of writers. I am fortunate to work with her and call her friend. Check out the heartfelt, wonderful books that Charlesbridge Publishing produces.

Gary Crespo designed the cover, and put up with my repeated tweaks and suggestions.

Wendy McDonald poured over every page of the manuscript multiple times, copyediting and checking the design. Its consistent, professional look is due to her.

Katie Ginder-Vogel did the final copyedit, but also has provided friendship and support to me for decades.

Thanks to Dave Pasquantonio, Heather Kelly, and Kristen Wixted, friends from the Writers' Loft in Sherborn, MA. From questions about software and marketing, to how to actually make this collection happen, they patiently explained everything I needed to know.

Thanks to dear friend Pam Vaughan for her support, excitement, and encouragement. Our conversations on long walks gave me the confidence I needed to make this happen.

Finally, I cannot thank my critique partners, Gary Crespo, Wendy McDonald, Megan Mullin, Danielle Renino, Phoebe Sinclair, and Annette Trossello, enough. For two decades they have supported me on my writing journey, and they didn't blink an eye when (after two glasses of wine) I put forth a "crazy idea" that we start our own press. They've all contributed time and expertise in making this happen. Now, Table for 7 has three books on schedule for 2021! I can't wait to see what the next two decades of our collaboration bring.

ABOUT THE AUTHOR

Erin M. Dionne writes all kinds of stories for all kinds of readers. She's published humorous novels for tweens, picture books for kids, short stories, flash fiction, and nonfiction. Her latest novel for young readers is *Secrets of a Fangirl* (Scholastic, 2019). She's written six other books for tweens, including *Lights, Camera, Disaster* (Scholastic, 2018) and *Moxie and the Art of Rule Breaking: A 14 Day Mystery. Moxie* was a 2014 Edgar Award finalist in the Juvenile category.

Her most recent picture book is *Balletball* (Charlesbridge, 2020). She is an Associate Professor of Liberal Arts at Montserrat College of Art, in Beverly, MA, and lives outside of Boston with her husband, two children, and a very indignant dog.

Bad Choices Make Good stories marks her first nonfiction collection. Find her online at erindionne.com.

ALSO BY ERIN M. DIONNE

Balletball

Secrets of a Fangirl

Captain's Log: Snowbound

CPSIA information can be obtained
at www.ICGtesting.com
Printed in the USA
LVHW112339050521
686648LV00006B/201